*The Challenge of Abundance*

# THE
# CHALLENGE
# OF
# ABUNDANCE

*by*

*ROBERT THEOBALD*

*Clarkson N. Potter, Inc./Publisher*

NEW YORK

*Library of Congress Catalog Card Number:* 61-11426

*First Edition*

# Contents

*To Nana*

# Preface

THE PURPOSE OF this preface is to inform the reader of the aim of this book. It was not written for, and would certainly infuriate, those who believe that the Western world has already developed the answers to all contemporary problems both at home and abroad. It *is* aimed at the reader who values Western traditions but who does not think that the economic, social, and political attitudes developed in earlier years will necessarily be suitable in today's conditions. This book sets out some of the implications of the continuing economic and social revolutions and suggests certain changes in policy that seem to be necessary.

One of the catch phrases of the 1960 election was "new frontiers." However, the complaint was general that neither of the candidates described even vaguely the areas that lay beyond these borders. An attempt has been made here to produce a very large-scale map of the new territory we will enter during the 1960's and later decades. Just as the first map of new physical terrain often turns out to be somewhat inaccurate when the land is more fully surveyed, some of the ideas and solutions proposed in this book are open to challenge. However, this very process could stimulate the basic discussion we so badly need.

Where are the economies of abundance? It is in America that abundance has developed most fully, but it is already raising challenges in many other countries. Abundance develops when an increase in the production of material goods raises new problems even while meeting our traditional goal of a higher material standard of living; this position has been reached or will soon be attained in many European countries. Examination of social comment in European countries reveals a preoccupation with the same problems that are now taking the center of the stage in America.

The argument in this book will certainly be dismissed by some on the ground that it ignores "realities." This is a polite way of saying that major reforms are impossible because of human selfishness. I can only reply that critics who use this argument ignore the fact that a new situation now exists, and that continuation of the old patterns of selfishness will ensure that mankind will not survive. With his continued existence at stake it seems possible that he may find ways to make the necessary changes. No realist can think that the chances of carrying out the needed reforms are very high; on the other hand, no human being should deny the possibility of success, for in so doing he denies the ability of man to adjust to changed conditions.

Other people will certainly be concerned that I have not consistently discussed the implications of the present cold-war struggle. This omission was dictated by our being concerned with what the West *should* do rather than with what it is forced to do. Such an approach would obviously be unrealistic if the cold-war were to remain a major factor in our calculations in coming decades. However, I do not believe that we can continue to accept the present position for an indefinite period, and I make suggestions for moving toward a new world order in the last two chapters.

I have continued to use the terms "rich" and "poor" to cover the groups of countries more usually designated as "developed" and "underdeveloped," as I have previously done in *The Rich and the Poor: A Study of the Economics of Rising*

*Expectations.* It seems to me that this dichotomy between rich and poor suggests more clearly the essential difference between these groups of countries than the terms "developed" and "underdeveloped." These latter terms seem to include the idea that the distinction is not only economic but also social and cultural. I have been encouraged in this decision by the increasing frequency of this usage. In addition, I have suggested that the term "transnational" be used to describe relations between states. I wish to distinguish by this usage between the present pattern of relations between sovereign states and a new world order that would transcend this concept.

This book was written using the work of literally hundreds of authors whose ideas I have absorbed through catholic reading in many fields. I have therefore been able to acknowledge my debt only to those whose influence on my thinking has been particularly direct and to those from whom I have quoted—this does not mean that I am unaware of the contribution of many others. Some of the ideas presented here were developed or refined in two groups set up under the auspices of the Society for International Development. Others were worked out when studying economic issues for General Electric. Miss Audrey Duckert and Walter Brown read the manuscript; their comments enabled me to iron out some particularly difficult problems. I, however, am fully responsible.

I take great pleasure in acknowledging my debt to Clarkson Potter, who made it possible for me to write this book and ensured by his comments that it would be far better than I could have made it without his help. Finally, my wife, Jean Scott, provided me with much of the information I have used and her critical comments prevented me from making many specific errors. Her contribution, however, cannot be detailed, for the whole book reflects our continuing discussion.

# Acknowledgment

I WOULD LIKE TO acknowledge permission to quote from the following sources: "The Subversion of Collective Bargaining," by Daniel Bell, in the March 1960 issue of *Commentary;* "Great American Scientists: The Biologists," by Francis Bello, in the June 1960 issue of *Fortune;* "America the Expendable," by Charlton Ogburn, Jr., in the August 1960 issue of *Harper's Magazine;* "Africa Needs Time," by Julius Nyerere in the March 27, 1960, issue of the *New York Times Magazine;* the booklet *A Bold New System—Basic Democracies,* produced by the Bureau of National Reconstruction, Government of Pakistan; the folder on giving to the United Nations by the Urbana-Champaign Friends; *New Frontiers for Professional Managers,* by Ralph J. Cordiner, 1956, McGraw-Hill Book Company, Inc.; and *The General Theory of Employment, Interest, and Money,* by John Maynard Keynes, 1936, Harcourt Brace & Company, Inc.

*The Challenge of Abundance*

# 1.

## *What Is the Challenge?*

A DEEP SENSE OF unease has been developing in the Western countries in the last decade. Despite the fulfillment and indeed the overfulfillment of many of the originally accepted postwar goals, there are few who feel that we can now relax. Although production and incomes have reached record levels, although a middle-class standard of living is being attained by an increasing proportion of the population of the West, there is still widespread economic dissatisfaction. In addition, many observers feel that the improvement in economic standards during the past fifteen years has been bought at a heavy social cost. They suggest that the attitudes necessary for the most rapid rate of growth are not those which encourage a meaningful life for the individual or a valid sense of community.

Even more disconcertingly, our successes have only revealed new difficulties. The experience has been similar to that of a mountain climber who reaches the top of the only peak visible to him to find that others, far higher, stretch as far as he can see. For example, it is only in the years since the war that we have realized the full extent of the dilemma in the poor countries, that we have begun to understand the obsolescence of all concepts of national sovereignty in a world with rapid communication and mutual destructive powers, that we have started to examine the dangers brought about by the continuing social and economic revolution. We have learned that the victory over poverty in the rich countries that is now in our grasp does not relieve us of all responsibility; that new problems we must try to solve have arisen.

Nineteen hundred and sixty was memorable for the beginning of a debate on "The National Purpose." However, few people felt that the resulting discussion greatly clarified the situation. For, while there was general agreement on the need to reconsider our way of life, it seems fair to say that few radically new policies were suggested, nor was there general agreement about which values were peripheral and which central to Western culture. The failure of these discussions to generate even a clear statement of the *issues,* despite the participation of many prominent leaders of opinion, demonstrated clearly our present position "Wandering between two worlds, one dead, the other powerless to be born." The object of this book is to examine the conditions in which we now live and to suggest the changes we must make if we are to deal with the alterations that our own actions have brought about. But more than this, its purpose is to suggest that we must develop a new *positive* philosophy if we are not to find our lives disrupted and destroyed by the very fruits of economic and scientific progress.

This book, like all syntheses, is a composite of many ideas. Certainly most of them are already acceptable to specialists in the various fields of study discussed. Nevertheless the approach employed here is not a common one, and it was therefore felt that the reader might benefit from a summary of the discussion. It is, of course, impossible to present more than an outline here: the supporting examples and argument will be found in each chapter.

Anyone who attempts to write about the future must be deeply conscious of his own limitations. There are too many uncertainties that make it impossible to "predict" events. It is only hoped that this book may provide a framework for discussion: that it will help to illuminate some of the important questions. Each new proposal made here should be considered tentative and open to further argument.

The first essential, if we are to determine the nature of the problems that beset us and the solutions that might be given to them, is to define the situation we face (Chapter 2). We must try to examine it free from the preconceptions inherited from previous theories. The primary value that distinguished the West from the poor countries in the past was its pursuit of economic growth. This acceptance of economic growth led to alterations in economic conditions, in political and social realities, and also in international relations. Economic growth is synonymous with change.

The business corporation has been the prime driving force behind economic development and change in the West in the twentieth century. Its research and development programs have increased productivity and made it possible for people to buy more goods. These same programs have led to a change in the distribution of the labor force from being predominantly agricultural, through a stage when a large proportion was employed in manufacturing, to today's position, when an ever-increasing number are employed in the service industries —entertainment, advertising, finance, distribution, etc. In addition, the actions of the company have increased the amount of goods people wish to buy, through the development of new products and attempts to stimulate new desires. The actions of business enterprises have changed the economy from a relatively static condition to one of being fully dynamic. More goods are made available for purchase each year, and more goods must therefore be bought if full employment is to be maintained.

This development of a high-production, high-consumption economy has deprived economic theories developed in earlier periods of much of their validity. We must develop new ones if we are to understand and control the economy today. Given our present economic and social system, the government must accept the responsibility of keeping the total effective demand for goods equal to the potential supply. In present conditions this means that it must ensure that consumer demand, investment expenditures, and government purchases do not fluctuate violently and that the total from the three sources is sufficient to allow the purchase of all the goods that can be supplied.

The real significance of the development of a high-production, high-consumption economy lies deeper. It allows, and indeed forces, us to re-examine certain basic theories by which we have lived in the past. In an economy of abundance, economic growth would not need to be given top priority; science could be used in such a way that it would increase rather than decrease the validity of human life. Similarly, we would need to re-examine the belief that the "invisible hand" of economic forces will automatically lead to a coincidence between private and social goals. These are the subjects examined in Chapters 3–10.

However, before we can discuss these matters satisfactorily, we must understand how the ideas of the social sciences, of Western philosophy, and even our linguistic habits tend to direct our thoughts along certain stylized lines (Chapter 3). Each country and group in society tends to look on its own values and way of life as *necessarily* right, while finding those of people in other societies either misguided or definitely wrong. We still have not understood the problems that arise when the values of two different countries come into contact, and usually into conflict. Nor have we really accepted that changes in conditions may make past theories completely inadequate.

One of the most important areas in which old theories are inhibiting the development of a viable society of abundance is our treatment of the distribution of income. This question of the *right* distribution of income was not discussed for several decades because of the economic theory stating that it *should* be determined by market forces: that any interference with these market forces was unwarranted and would actually reduce the welfare of society.

This theory is now inadequate for two reasons. First, it is obviously essential to its application that one should be able to determine how much each person is actually contributing to the enterprise—what is the value of his activity. For unless this condition is met it is impossible to decide how much he should actually receive. In today's closely integrated world, where the value of one person's work depends in large part on the over-all operation of the economy, the contribution of any single individual to the volume of production cannot be meaningfully determined. Even more important, however, is the fact that with increasing abundance in the rich countries we can pay less attention to the effect of the distribution of income on the rate of economic growth, and we can give far more weight to social justice.

As the distribution of income is one of the major factors
determining the nature of society, Chapters 4–6 are devoted
to a discussion of the forces that have affected and will change
this distribution. In Chapter 4 we discuss the efficacy and
relevance of the currently accepted method of changing the
division of income—labor-management bargaining. We find
that the use of power has permitted the unionized worker to
obtain a very large share of the increase in resources that has
become available in postwar years, and that this increase has
been achieved at the expense of those with fixed incomes and
certain types of savings.

In addition, the labor-management bargaining process is
shown to lead to many serious conflicts—most notably between
the long-range and the short-range interests of labor. In the
short run the union must be interested in obtaining the largest possible increase in benefits. However, the long-term effects of this increase will be unfavorable to the prospects of
those in the union, for the increased payments for wages make
it profitable for management to install more equipment, and
thus cause a decrease in the labor force.

There was a period in the postwar years when labor and
management "combined" to decide on the size of wage increase and passed the cost of these increases onto the consumer by raising prices. Developing resistance from the public has led many companies to abandon this approach in recent
years. In some cases this change has simply led to a hardening
of management attitudes toward labor demands. But some
companies have evolved new approaches that may have more
far-reaching results. Several corporations now claim that only
they have the right to determine the proper distribution of
benefits among stockholders, suppliers, labor, and the general
public. These companies argue that the only role of the union
is to provide them with the information they will require to

carry out this process efficiently. They completely reject the past concept of the union as an independent agent that should try to gain the best possible bargain for the workers it represents. The strike against General Electric by the International Union of Electrical Workers in the fall of 1960 can be understood only in terms of the different concepts of the proper role for the union advanced by the two sides.

It has long been one of the basic tenets of Western economic thought that the distribution of income should be determined by market forces and labor-management bargaining. In particular, it has been assumed that the government should not intervene in the economy (Chapter 5). In today's world, where government action customarily accounts for a quarter or more of the spending in a country, this approach is unrealistic. Government action will necessarily affect the distribution of income: it cannot avoid helping some industries and hindering others; it will necessarily benefit some members of society by its actions and damage the interests of others. The demand for government "neutrality" is now unrealistic. This fact is demonstrated by examining how government activity inevitably affects the profitability and efficiency of various types of transport. For example, the need for progress in military aircraft has allowed the development of a subsonic commercial jet and placed in prospect a supersonic commercial aircraft for the end of the 1960's. Meanwhile the development of a 200-m.p.h. fixed-rail form of transportation lags, although the technical problems involved in its development are almost certainly far less difficult.

Many necessary services cannot be carried out on an individual basis; only the community as a whole can finance them. Our present tax systems are, however, both unjust and overloaded. We must therefore reconsider the means that governments should use to raise funds for their necessary activities (Chapter 6). We must re-examine how government should obtain its funds in an economy of abundance. We have assumed in the past that balanced budgets are essential for the health of a nation, that a country cannot afford to allow governments to *create* funds except in an emergency. These beliefs must be discussed in the light of today's—and tomorrow's —realities.

Our systems of taxation are based on beliefs that are no longer valid. Our methods often lack logic, for many types of taxation were introduced to raise money in emergencies but later were hallowed by their continued existence and are now accepted as "right." In addition, we have a preference for direct income taxes as opposed to indirect sales taxes—an approach reflecting conditions in a nineteenth-century economy.

A major change in approach is needed if governments are to compete effectively with industry in raising the funds they require. The present system of pricing goods allows the corporation in effect to "tax" the consumer. The firm sets its prices at a level that will not only cover its production costs but will also allow it to expand. The corporation levies a hidden tax, its existence not even suspected by the great majority of the population. On the other hand, most government taxes are not only open but are aggressively displayed. For example, most sales taxes are not automatically included in the cost of the product but added separately at the time of the purchase.

The threads of the argument are brought together in Chapter 7 to suggest the necessary future evolution of the economy. A preliminary objection is first answered. It might be suggested that our present system should not be altered because of its success in the past. It is shown that it is the very success of the system that has made change necessary, that the growth of the economy has made it possible to satisfy private needs to a great extent and has therefore made community needs relatively more urgent.

The discussion of the right distribution of income is then carried further. It is shown that, in today's conditions, market forces will not lead to a satisfactory distribution of the national income. Also, individuals can no longer assure by their own efforts that a job will be available for them in the economy.

We have a duty to ensure that nobody suffers through the operation of an economy that the individual can no longer control. Indeed, as market prices do not reflect real values, it is possible that society should subsidize the student, the artist, the dreamer, the visionary, and perhaps even the writer—recognizing that many activities that are necessary to the vitality and indeed the survival of society will not be adequately recompensed by the working of the free-enterprise system.

This section of the book, dealing with the economies of the rich countries, ends with a challenge to the "mythology" of growth. It is shown that our conventional methods of calculation overstate the benefits to be derived from economic growth while understating or even ignoring the disadvantages.

Mankind has brought an ever-changing world into existence, but he has still given insufficient attention to its full meaning. We have not adjusted our educational and political systems to the effect of change, nor have we fully faced the philosophical implications of an ever-changing, ever-developing world. Our educational systems are still primarily geared to inculcating past theories rather than to teaching students "how" to think so that they can make sense for themselves of their own situations (Chapter 8).

Education today can be meaningful only if we accept that

it must be a lifelong process. The development of knowledge is now so rapid we cannot be content to educate the child until he gains his high-school diploma, his M.A., or his Ph.D. and then leave him to fend for himself. We must find ways in which each person can continue to learn throughout his life. It may be necessary for the idea of sabbatical years—a period away from one's normal duties—to become general in not only the academic but also the professional and industrial worlds. This will, of course, raise new problems—the educational relationship for older people must be one of mutual respect between the practical "student" and the theoretical "teacher" rather than follow the traditional teacher-student relationship.

There is no "ideal" pattern for political control of a nation: all systems have both advantages and disadvantages (Chapter 9). The ideal of democracy is the best that has been devised, but its application raises very major difficulties. We should not assume that the precise mechanisms developed for the application of democratic methods in the past will necessarily be suitable for a society of abundance.

Indeed, there may well be one major disadvantage to the present methods of control used in the West. The democratic countries have relied on the use of power in settling disputes to a greater extent than many of the poor countries. We have allowed one group to bring pressure to bear on others, and have felt that the resulting decisions were just—or at least justified. Thus the West permits strikes and lockouts: labor and management are legally permitted to pit their economic strength against each other. The acceptance of power as a method of settling disputes is far less complete in some other cultures, which try to resolve conflicts by negotiated compromises between differing points of view or have developed their concept of law so that it covers more situations than in the West. The Western use of power rather than compromise is far from "ideal," for it very often leads to considerable bitterness that antagonizes both sides for long periods and continues even after the dispute has been "technically" terminated .

The West has many power centers: some of the most important are the management of corporations. These groups have developed far more of the characteristics of a "government" than has been generally realized. For a variety of reasons they have almost complete control over the actions of employees: in addition they have taxing power over all those who buy their goods. This power is subject to few sanctions: in most cases the directors of a corporation are not really subject to any form of outside control. Despite this lack most observers would probably agree that the directors of companies usually act in the interests of their companies rather than try to benefit themselves. Or, more strictly speaking, the interests of the individual within the firm have been made to correspond with those of the corporation. We need to consider the application of these facts to government activity. The present emphasis in government work is to ensure that each official's actions are subject to checks and balances in order to curb the use of unjustified power. We must examine whether we can develop a set of values that would discourage the government official from using the advantages of his position to favor himself.

We have been dealing predominantly with "means" in the discussion so far, although some ideas about the proper ends are obviously implicit in the argument. Chapter 10 discusses what the goals of Western society should be. It is hardly necessary to say that this subject has too many facets to be treated completely in this book; only some of the broader aspects of the subject can be discussed and some of the cruder fallacies dismissed. Our main need is to take charge of our destiny once more: to make sure that we control the use of scientific developments rather than follow posthaste wherever science may open new possibilities. Man must use scientific knowledge; he must not be used by it.

It has always been argued that science is neither good nor bad—but that it can be used for both good and bad ends. This argument is valid only as long as man examines the potential of scientific discoveries and decides for himself whether they are good or evil. Today the development of science is leading man to take steps that will be harmful for him. This is only too obvious in the case of military weapons—it has recently been suggested that the "logic" of events may even force humanity to move underground if it wishes to survive. However, the danger also exists—if less obviously—that the development of computer and automation techniques could turn man into efficient robots.

What is the basic value of the West? It is a concern for freedom—for the basic right of each individual to make up his own mind. But despite concern with this problem the record is not completely satisfactory. The West has often interpreted freedom as license. In addition, the process of industrialization has restricted the areas in which meaningful decisions can be made—institutional constraints limit the range of choice for most people.

Real freedom is possible only when man knows the goal toward which he wants to move and has the necessary information that will allow him to make the right choices in particular situations. Freedom is limited when the individual is unable to make his own decisions in the areas that are most important. Despite the potential freedom afforded by the rate of economic growth, our economic system does not allow most people the freedom to develop their lives as they think fit, nor is it very successful in providing the necessary information to allow man to make a *meaningful* choice. Economic developments *could* give fuller freedom to those within the rich countries, but the present methods of organization do not allow the development of this freedom. In actual fact industrial civilization sets up *more* constraints rather than less for the great majority of the population. It must be our concern to find ways of allowing the potential freedom available from economic growth and the increase in knowledge to be realized.

However, it is only one third of the world that is in the happy position of being able to reduce the importance given to economic growth, for it is in only one third of the world that a reasonable standard of living has been attained—or can be attained—in the next generation. The remaining two thirds of the world is poor and often getting poorer despite the misleading impression given by national income statistics, which exaggerate progress and minimize regression or even make it appear as an improvement (Chapter 11). The poor countries are beset by a multitude of immediate problems that must be solved. They will therefore be unable to grant all the liberties that a high material standard of living has made possible in the developed areas.

The problems of the poor countries have been described many times. These nations have low incomes, rising expenditures, and rising populations—their survival therefore demands a rapid rate of economic growth. But the poor countries believe that this economic growth must not be allowed to destroy their culture—that it must be a means to validate their way of life and not to undermine it. They believe that the pattern of economic growth in the West has led to unrestrained individualism, which has removed the real meaning from life.

The rich countries must therefore re-examine the philosophy that lies behind their aid to the poor countries. Up to the present time we have largely concentrated on securing the maximum rate of growth and have felt justified in riding roughshod over any "cultural" opposition. We must look for a way of using economic growth as a means of preserving the validity of life rather than as an end in itself. We must not forget that there is undoubtedly a fairly close correlation between economic growth—as it has been achieved in the past—and an increase in social ills.

The problem is not simple. Economic growth in the poor countries will require major changes in social systems. Present attitudes toward work, saving, and family size all guarantee that the rate of growth will be inadequate at the present time. Thus economic growth cannot be attained without some social disruption. The task of these countries is to decide on the pattern of society they wish to attain and then work toward it. Economic growth will be important in this process but it cannot be given absolute priority.

The rich countries will have to reconsider some other basic beliefs (Chapter 12). We argue that the present system of international trade is not only convenient but also *morally* right. We have failed to realize that the particular pattern of conditions in the rich and the poor countries enables the rich countries to sell their goods at a relatively high price while forcing the poor to sell theirs at relatively low prices. The rich countries gain more advantage from present patterns of trade than the poor. The terms of trade have been moving in favor of the rich countries and against the poor over the last decades.

We must also realize that both the pace of change and the very pattern of development have damaged the interests of the poor countries. For example, the profits derived from the introduction into the rich countries of synthetic rubber were far smaller than the losses incurred by the producers of *natural* rubber.

The rich countries must try to aid the poor in all the ways that are open to them. They must change the rules applied in international trade, they must encourage private investment abroad, and they will need to increase international aid. We must reconsider the whole concept of international economic relations, realizing that our present methods are only manmade and can therefore be changed to meet new conditions. One example might be given here. In previous centuries both the internal economies of countries and external trade were based on gold. It was long ago recognized that the extension of credit was essential to the satisfactory operation of the internal economies of countries—we have still applied this lesson only very hesitatingly in international economic relations.

We live in a time of change, and we will survive only if we recognize that we must alter our institutions to meet this change (Chapter 13). The dangers that result from our unwillingness to accept the need for evolution in our ideals is most striking in international affairs. Each country still believes that its views are right and that all those who disagree with it must necessarily be wrong. Because of the increase in the rapidity of communication these conflicting views clash with increasing directness at a time when war would lead to mutual destruction.

We have to develop new ways of looking at the world; we have to recognize that two countries may both be genuinely convinced that their policies are right and that those of others are wrong. We have to realize that the impossibility of meaningful victory in any war has deprived power politics of its real sanction—and therefore ultimately of all meaning. We have to understand that in today's world self-preservation is possible only if we can find ways to compromise our differences and if we adopt a policy of mutual concessions. If we are to do this, we must ensure that each country understands the aims of all others. The old sanction of breaking off diplomatic relations with other countries in times of disagreement no longer corresponds to present needs, for we cannot afford to be unaware of the aims and objectives of other countries. We will have to compromise our differences because we have no way of imposing our will on others: the most basic need will be accurate information about the aims of others.

Although compromise and concessions will require a change in our institutions, there is need for an even greater alteration in ideals. Mankind must cease to be loyal to its country "right or wrong" and adopt a wider commitment (Chapter 14). We must seek a policy that will be best for the world as a whole rather than for one particular country. If this is to be possible, we must provide a way in which those of like mind can meet together and build a forum for their views. I believe that this can be done only by creating a class of world citizens who will deliberately reject narrow national interests. In this way we will eventually be able to rise above the present international disorder to an ordered transnational system.

**PART I**

*The Economic Challenge*

# 2.

## The Development of Abundance

ONE OF THE major distinctive contributions of Western society to the evolution of values has been its acceptance of economic growth as a very important goal in life. Priority has been given to the task of securing a high material standard of living in the belief that success in this area would ensure the "good life" for *all* members of society. It was undoubtedly America that first gave prime importance to this aim of economic development, but in the postwar years Europe, Japan, Australia, New Zealand, and Russia have also made growth their overriding concern. Also, many of the poor countries have now accepted this goal. However, their present position and problems are so different that we must distinguish their difficulties from those of the rich countries.

Although the West is committed to economic growth, it has still not realized that economic growth is synonymous with change and that if we value economic growth we must accept continuous change as its inevitable concomitant. Indeed, the West's willingness to accept economic growth as its most important goal rests in part on the fact that economic theory has consistently underemphasized the unpleasant implications of growth—the fact that it inevitably disrupts present methods, principles, and values. Economic growth occurs through change—change from using one expensive material to using another that is cheaper, change from using manpower to produce goods to using machinery, change from one supplier of products to another. Economic theory has tended to write off the hardship that results from these changes as the necessary costs of progress.

Of course, lip service is paid to the need for change, and there are many areas in which the disruption caused by alterations is accepted. It is generally agreed that the obligation of a corporation to any of its employees can be terminated at any time—however long they may have worked for the firm and whatever the effect on their lives may be. Opinion also supports the right of government compulsorily to take over land if it is required for certain public purposes. People have generally accepted that the pursuit of economic advantage will often require movement from one place to another.

The United States talks about change as *the* condition for economic growth, but has largely limited its acceptance of change to the *economic* field. The institutional structures and educational processes of Western countries are set up in such a way that it is normally assumed that the past is the proper guide to policy unless it can be proved conclusively that a new course would be better. It is not yet realized that revolutionary economic and scientific changes often create presumptive evidence that the techniques applied in the past are no longer suitable.

It is this difference between economic change and change in other areas that has allowed the corporation to be the first, and most successful, institution to break through the barrier of resistance to new ideas. The corporation that wishes to expand *must* view change as necessary, for new products and new methods of selling are the only way to obtain continued growth and profits. This does not mean, of course, that there are no vested interests in the corporation, no cliques or pressure groups seeking to ensure better treatment for one department than for another, no blocks to the progress of new ideas. It does mean that the corporation can be successful only if it is aware of the need for "uniqueness" in its products; if it can keep ahead of its competition.

Firms can obtain high prices and good profits only if they can convince the consumer that they have something to sell that no other firm can match. Many advertising, packaging, and research and development expenditures are devoted to this end. Each firm tries to build and retain customer loyalty for itself. Each firm must try to convince the customer that only *its* own brand can offer a particular set of advantages. In this way it can raise its price above that which would be possible if it were competing directly with all brands in a single market. It tries in fact to create a separate market for its own goods.

The classic example of the ability of firms to differentiate their products in the eyes of the public is the cigarette industry. Although it is generally agreed that there is no major difference—many observers would say *no* difference—in certain types of cigarettes, each company tries and succeeds in keeping smokers loyal to its own brand. People are known not to smoke if they cannot get one particular brand, and to walk blocks to obtain the type they usually smoke. However, when confronted with a test in which their own type of cigarette is not identified they are usually unable to pick out their habitual choice. The same unswerving loyalty has been developed for other types of goods.

The increased expenditures on advertising, research and development, and model changes that are necessary to stay ahead of competitors have cut heavily into the profitable life of goods. Products that used to sell for twenty-five years now often count on no more than five. In the volatile pharmaceutical and electronic fields the period is often as short as six months. A very large proportion of the profits of even the longest-established corporations comes from products developed since 1945; while some of the most successful firms today are concerned, not only with products developed since 1945, but with whole fields of manufacture that have come into existence since the end of World War II.

The rate of expenditure on research and development has also limited the life of machinery. In the past the choice between types of equipment was based on their expected physical life and their cost. Now an additional factor must be considered; firms are no longer concerned only with the period a machine will last, but primarily with its useful economic life. The continuing development of new types of machinery makes obsolescence the controlling factor in many purchases; tools must often be scrapped although they are still in perfect operating condition. This development has necessarily led to a change in purchasing policies: expensive special-purpose machinery is being avoided, and firms try to purchase tools that can be adapted to their changing needs.

That the rate of growth of research and development expenditures is one of the major factors leading to the obsolescence of both products and machinery is still not generally realized. From a total of $100 million spent by government, industry, and the universities for these purposes in America in 1920, expenditure rose to $300 million in 1930, $900 million in 1941, $2,900 million in 1950, and $10,200 million in 1958. Expenditures on research and development have been rising almost seven times as fast as national income in recent years, and this rate of increase seems likely to continue.

Together with the rise in the amount of money spent on research and development has come a revolution in the techniques used for studying problems. The development of new ideas is no longer a hit-and-miss affair. Research is usually directed toward a particular goal. The Stanford Research Institute expressed this idea in the following way: "Someone has said that in recent times we have invented the art of systematic invention. Organized scientific research and development, which has become a great industry in the last few decades, is itself one of the most significant social inventions of the twentieth century. It is unlocking the secrets of nature and putting the knowledge to practical use at an unprecedented rate. Also we have invented the art of systematic innovation . . . ; a large part of the business skill in some modern corporations is devoted to launching new products and processes. . . ." It is now even possible to predict the areas in which break-throughs are expected; research is planned and not haphazard. Indeed, the greatest danger today is that we will forget that the really revolutionary new ideas cannot by their very nature be blocked out in advance.

An increasing amount of support is given to projects that can point to a definite aim and a probability of success. Far less support can be found for the blue-sky approach, the reexamination of the fundamentals of a subject with no specific conclusion in view. There is an implicit assumption here that the frontiers of knowledge have been finally reached and that the remaining work is in mapping the detailed topography of each subject. In fact, many of the most eminent students of the physical and the social sciences feel that the basic theories in many areas are still inadequate to explain facts completely. Indeed, many social scientists would go further —they feel that progress will be possible only when their now fragmented disciplines are reintegrated.

The greatest increase in research and development expenditures has been made by the industrial firm. Up to the present time, industrial research and development work has usually been done by a single firm. But there have now been a significant number of occasions when the complexity and cost of a project have forced collaboration between competitive firms to suggest that this may be an increasingly common pattern in coming years. Such techniques have most often been used for military contracts, but firms have also worked together to develop civilian goods. For example, thirty companies pooled their resources in order to specify color TV in detail, check their theories, assure themselves that all the necessary apparatus was practical, and sell the whole thing to the government and nation. The future development of guidance techniques for automobiles where accidents will be prevented by electrical apparatus in the road will probably require a similar grouping. It has been seriously suggested by at least one authority that the only sensible pattern for developing a supersonic commercial jet would be the combination of the engineering talent available on both sides of the Atlantic. Indeed, the very fact that it is often possible to predict the results of research is likely to quicken this trend. As long as research was a chancy affair, firms could see little advantage in banding together. Now that the aims and even the results of research can often be predicted, cost- and profit-sharing arrangements become more feasible.

It is this process of research and development that allowed the appearance of the present industrial system where man co-operates with a large quantity of equipment to produce goods: without machinery output would shrink to a minute fraction of its present level. But this is not all. In the years since the war we have learned to produce machines that can make "efficient" decisions, that can work in many cases more rapidly and with fewer errors than man himself. This has opened new possibilities—but perhaps not so many as some naïve commentators would have us believe. We return to this subject in Chapter 10.

The process of mechanization and automation revolutionized the distribution of the labor force. As productivity increased, fewer men were needed in areas that had previously required most of the energy of the population. The first step was for labor to move out of agriculture. Before the Western countries developed economically, about three quarters of the labor force was engaged in agriculture. Today only 10 per cent of the labor force is employed on farms in America, and the figures are similar in Europe. The labor force that was moved out of agriculture found employment in manufacturing and in the service industries.

The first result of the agricultural revolution was to allow increased employment in manufacturing and therefore a larger production of goods. However, we now seem to be entering a new era. Despite the continuing increase in manufacturing, the number of people employed in this field appears to have reached a peak, at least in the United States. Total employment in the manufacturing industries was 17,500,000 at the height of the 1953–54 boom, 17,100,000 at the height of the 1956–57 boom, and only 16,500,000 at the height of the 1959–60 boom. There was an even more rapid decline in the number employed in agriculture—employment fell from 7,500,000 in 1950 to 5,800,000 in 1959.

The people forced out of manufacturing and agriculture had to find work elsewhere. In addition, there was a continuing increase in the labor force that also had to be absorbed if unemployment were not to increase. These people could move only into the service industries. However, employment in these industries, taken as a whole, has not been increasing rapidly enough to allow everybody to find jobs. As a result *un*employment increased throughout the 1950's—rising from less than 3 per cent in the boom of 1952 to around 5 per cent throughout the boom of 1959–60. If a further rise in unemployment is to be avoided in the 1960's, the rate of increase in job openings will have to be considerably augmented, for the rate of increase in the labor force in America in the 1960's is expected to be double that of the 1950's.

The problem of providing employment for all those who need it may well become more difficult in coming years. Firms are only now beginning to apply computer techniques in offices and thus are starting to reduce office staffs, which have increased in the last decade. A report by Representative Elmer Holland suggests that machines will eliminate 4 million office and clerical jobs in the next five years. Potential changes in distribution techniques can also be expected to cut into the rate of increase in employment. We will see in later chapters that this does not mean that unemployment will necessarily result, for policies can be adopted that will avoid it. It does mean that we will be able, and indeed we will be forced, to re-examine what are the best economic policies in a society of growing abundance.

The task of providing employment for everybody will be complicated by alterations in the demand for various types of labor. Despite the decline in the total number of people employed in manufacturing, the number of white-collar workers has been increasing—the percentage of white-collar workers compared to total manufacturing employment has increased from 20 per cent in 1953 to 25 per cent in 1960. Such a change has, of course, many favorable effects. As Adam Smith stated in the eighteenth century: "The man whose whole life is spent in performing a few simple operations, of which the effects too are, perhaps, always the same or very nearly the same, has no occasion to exert his understanding or to exercise his invention in finding out expedients for removing difficulties which never occur. He naturally . . . becomes as stupid and ignorant as it is possible for a human creature to become. The torpor of his mind renders him, not only incapable of relishing or bearing a part in any rational conversation, but of conceiving any generous, noble, or tender sentiment and, consequently, of forming any just judgment concerning many even of the ordinary duties of private life." Today the assembly line is only part of man's life, but its effects are still unhappy.

If job opportunities decline for blue-collar workers, we must make sure that the number of people seeking this type of work also decreases. There seems to be a real danger that many of those who are now working at unskilled jobs or who would normally accept this type of work on leaving school will be unable to find suitable employment in the future. We must therefore make certain that we alter our educational system so as to match the supply of labor with the type of jobs available. We have an opportunity to get rid of the drudgery of unskilled labor: this opportunity will turn into a tragedy if we continue to educate people in such a way that they will be able to carry out only unskilled labor.

What are the forces that are altering the demand for labor and the types of labor the economy requires? Why is the firm and the farm—which is increasingly a food factory—installing more and more machinery and using fewer and fewer men? The essential reason is that the continuing rise in wages makes it more advantageous to replace labor by machinery. The rise in labor costs and the increasing efficiency of machinery cause many jobs performed more cheaply by human labor in the past to cost less if machines are used.

This, however, is only one side of the picture. There is another important effect that follows the continuing increase in wages and salaries: people can afford to purchase additional goods. Such a statement is obvious and commonplace. However, it is not so generally accepted that this rise in potential consumers' expenditures means that we can no longer rely on the stability of actual spending in coming decades; indeed, it may well be that changes in consumption expeditures will be a major cause of cyclical fluctuations in the future. As long as the consumer could afford to buy only the necessary food, clothing, and shelter and had little left over for "discretionary spending"—purchases of nonessentials—only a decrease in his income could cause him to curtail his rate of spending. As consumers now spend a large proportion of their income on nonessentials, this stability can no longer be guaranteed. *Fortune* magazine, in the *Markets of the Sixties* analyzed how much of present consumers' income could be considered available for luxuries. The article suggested that, if one assumed that $4000 per family was needed for reasonable minimum standards of living in the United States at the present time, 60 per cent of all families earned more than this amount and the total volume of income above this figure amounted to $135,000,000,000. Projecting these figures into the future, the article suggested that more than half of all disposable personal income would be discretionary by 1970.

Some flexibility in expenditure has, of course, always existed, but before World War II it was clearly reasonable to believe that people would not reduce their purchases unless a decline in income forced them to do so. Today there is no reason why consumers should behave mechanistically in response to changes in income; they may themselves initiate changes. Consumers might decide that they wished to delay their purchases. Such a shift might take place at the beginning of a depression as people came to fear that they might be thrown out of their jobs and that they would therefore need money more than goods. Indeed, such a shift might occur even before a recession developed because people feared one might occur; this development would then either help to cause or actually initiate the depression. An analysis of the 1957–58 recession suggests that a decline in the demand for consumer durables—cars, refrigerators, power tools—was one of the major factors leading to its occurrence. Purchases of consumer durables started to fall in the second quarter of 1957, before the recession had really developed, and they continued to decline throughout the recession even though total incomes fell very little. The shift away from durables to other types of purchases, which required less labor to produce, was sufficient to worsen considerably the effect of the depression.

There is a second possibility, which has been very little discussed. The desire of the consumer for additional goods and a higher standard of living might decline. People would then come to spend less time and effort augmenting their incomes. It is clear that a change in attitudes has already occurred in the case of cars—the importance of the prestige factor in purchases has been declining. The compact car and many of the small imported cars are bought as a means of transport without much concern for status. Many commentators claim that the contempt for material goods is already more widely spread than is generally realized and that a real revolution in this field can be expected within a relatively limited time.

We must pay more attention to the possibility of variation in consumers' behavior than we have in the past. As soon as we look closely at this question, we find that the existence of a large volume of consumer credit represents a major potential danger to the economy. The danger, however, is not that the amount of credit outstanding is larger than the economy can support—it can support far more. The danger arises from the fact that the consumer might decide that he wished to rid himself of the debt burden, and this would cause the development of a major slump.

It is changes in expenditure that are important in determining the evolution of the economy. Thus, if total demand increases, manufacturers will produce the extra goods demanded. But there will be further effects. The additional people who are hired to produce these goods will spend a large proportion of their newly earned money. This will lead to a further increase in demand. Thus an initial increase in demand will lead to a far more substantial rise in total spending, which may be of the order of three or four times the original increase. (This assumes, of course, that productive capacity is available to meet the additional demand.) Similarly, a decrease in expenditure will usually lead to a far larger downward movement in total production. Thus, any decrease in the amount of consumer credit extended can cause considerable effects on total production through its "multiplier" effects. Increases and decreases in investment and government expenditure will have a similar effect.

When the recent experience of the United States is examined from this point of view, we can see that even in the 1950's consumer credit was a major destabilizing force. The amount of credit outstanding expanded during the boom, and credit tended to remain stable or even decline during a slump; the effect of consumers' credit was to increase the magnitude of cyclical fluctuations and perhaps even to initiate them. Thus consumer credit rose some four billion dollars in the boom year 1952 and about six billion dollars in 1955 and 1959. On the other hand, the amount of consumer credit outstanding hardly changed in 1954 and 1958, both recession years.

We must reconsider the causes of depressions. It is now recognized that they result from changes in expenditure—whether by government, firms, or consumers. Economists have paid most attention, in the past, to fluctuations in investment. However, if we compare expenditures by consumers with the amount of investment at the present time, we will see that in an affluent economy small changes in consumers' attitudes can have more serious repercussions than a major change in business attitudes toward investment. A 10-per-cent alteration in the volume of gross business investment will represent a decline of only seven billion dollars in spending; a 10-per-cent alteration in consumer spending would mean a change of some thirty-five billion dollars in the volume of demand. Thus a 3-per-cent alteration in consumers' expenditure would have much the same effect on the operation of the economy as a 10-per-cent variation in investment.

The possibility that fluctuations in consumers' attitudes rather than in investment will be the main cause of cyclical fluctuations is increased by recent alterations in business actions. In the years since the war the larger firms have realized that if the general trend of activity is upward—and it has now been generally accepted that this is the case in all the rich countries—it is unwise for them to make major reductions in investment simply because of a recession. This change in the reaction to recessions has been one of the major factors in preventing any of the postwar downturns from developing into major slumps. In particular this alteration

in attitudes kept the 1957–58 recession from being as serious
as many observers feared. Even before the recession began,
there was a considerable amount of unused capacity. Nevertheless, there was no real slump in the rate of investment,
which only fell from sixty-seven billion dollars to fifty-five
billion.

A further factor limits the willingness of firms to reduce
their expenditures on investment during a recession at the
present time. We have seen that there has been a rapid rise
in research and development expenditures in recent years,
with a consequent increase in the rate at which machinery
becomes obsolescent. Many firms find it essential to continue to purchase machinery to maintain their competitive
position even if they already have considerable surplus capacity. Thus the low operating rate of the steel mills during much of 1960 did not lead to a drastic reduction in
investment.

The need to find ways to control fluctuations in consumption expenditures rather than in investment is one of
the many changes that will be necessary as we move from
an economy of scarcity to an economy of abundance. In the
past our whole economic system has been postulated on the
existence of scarcity, and the production of goods has had a
high priority. In an economy of abundance it would be possible largely to take goods for granted: they would simply
be available. We have failed to comprehend the extent of
the leap we must make. The revolution required in our thinking is as great as when we changed from considering the
world as static and unchanging to thinking of it as a process
we can affect by our purposeful action.

Because of our obsession with scarcity we pose our problems in terms of either-or: the celebrated statement "guns
or butter" is always being repeated. But the error of the

1950's has been that we have not used the resources available to increase production. We must realize that there is no task America or the West wants to do that it cannot carry out. We hear that we cannot "afford" new subways, good schools, police forces, or housing. We can afford them if we want them enough and are willing to change our institutions so as not to hamper our desires. We will have to find ways of getting money to those who are still in need—even in America over 10 per cent of the population is believed to have an inadequate diet. We will have to find new ways of supporting community needs.

Given a vista of increasing abundance, we must reconsider the priority of various tasks—in particular our need for a faster rate of growth. Commentators differ greatly on the adequacy of our present rate of growth and the advantages we should seek to obtain from it. The majority of those in Western countries would willingly accept a more rapid rate of growth of the national income; indeed for many the rate of growth is *the* measurement of the success of a country. This unlimited commitment to growth is, however, often based on a lack of awareness of its inevitable concomitants —the pressure to buy new goods, the constant movement and change necessary if economic growth is to continue, the overturn of old and valued systems and landmarks. We will see in a later chapter that our methods of measuring economic growth have made its benefits appear greater than they often are.

Others who are more moderate in their commitment to growth as an ultimate value still claim that a far faster rate is necessary to achieve certain goals: in particular to attain a higher standard of living. However, there has been a notable development in the way this goal is stated in the last few years—a development that can be traced in large part to

John Galbraith's book *The Affluent Society*. It is now often suggested that additional resources are more urgently required to meet community needs for police, schools, education, slum clearance, control of air and water pollution rather than to satisfy additional private desires.

A few writers and thinkers accept the need for greater expenditures on public goals, but suggest that the economic system that has developed in the West will provide the needed economic growth almost automatically. They argue that the values of the corporation will lead to continued development and that we can therefore begin to concentrate our search for fulfillment in other directions. They suggest that the Western countries can quadruple their standards of living and reduce the work week to about fifteen hours within the lifetime of the generation now being educated. They argue that in these circumstances we should search more ardently for ways of making life meaningful rather than for ways of increasing material comfort. Many of them would suggest that we cannot ever "satisfy" our material wants as long as we *concentrate* upon them, for our wants can always run ahead of our means.

# 3.

## The Social Sciences: Help or Hindrance?

BELIEFS OF THE West, like those of all other world areas, can be traced back to their historical origins. We have already seen that the West has given greater importance to the goal of economic growth. But the task of achieving economic growth would have been far more difficult if new economic theories had not developed around the end of the eighteenth century. These theories can be summarized in two statements. First, it was argued that there was an inevitable concordance between private and community goals. Second, it was stated that it was both necessary and just to allow market forces to determine the distribution of income.

The West is unwilling to admit that it is largely the social commentator and the social scientist who have molded our

*37*

present world. Keynes, one of the most influential economists
of the twentieth century, set down perhaps the final word on
this subject. ". . . the ideas of economists and political philosophers, both when they are right and when they are wrong,
are more powerful than is commonly understood. Indeed the
world is ruled by little else. Practical men, who believe themselves to be quite exempt from any intellectual influences,
are usually the slave of some defunct economist. Madmen in
authority, who hear voices in the air, are distilling their
frenzy from some academic scribbler of a few years back. I
am sure that the power of vested interests is vastly exaggerated compared with the gradual encroachment of ideas. Not,
indeed, immediately, but after a certain interval; for in the
field of economic and political philosophy there are not many
who are influenced by new theories after they are twenty-five
or thirty years of age, so that the ideas which civil servants
and politicians and even agitators apply to current events
are not likely to be the newest. But, soon or late, it is ideas,
not vested interests, which are dangerous for good or evil."

Most of the theories of the social scientist have been developed by his use of the "scientific method": he has taken
over the methods and relations used in the physical sciences
and tries to examine man's actions using the same techniques.
The stated aims of the physical and the social sciences are
indeed very similar. Their object is to reduce the overwhelming diversity and complexity of reality to simple theoretical
regularities so that events can be understood and, if possible,
the future predicted on the basis of the laws discovered. Two
steps are generally considered necessary in the evolution of
a theory. First, observation of the facts or phenomena to be
described, and, second, the formulation of a theory that will
cover all the observed facts. It can then be tested by using it
for purposes of prediction: as long as it gives valid results, it

remains useful. However, if exceptions are found, it should be modified so that it will cover all the observed facts.

All observers agree that it is this scientific method that has allowed the physical sciences to explain an ever-increasing part of the physical universe. The process of classification and observation has made it possible to develop wider and wider theories. However, if we look back only four or five centuries, we find that the effective use of the scientific method is relatively new. The nature of the physical world in the fifteenth century was still an emotional subject, and attacks on accepted beliefs were liable to lead to ostracism or even death. For example, the reconstruction of beliefs that occurred when Magellan sailed around the world was not accomplished without considerable conflict. Today similar revolutions in scientific concepts are accepted calmly, for we regard scientific truth more or less dispassionately.

The social sciences are still hampered by the reactions that made progress in the physical sciences difficult in earlier centuries. Arguments in the social sciences cannot be confined to matters of fact and logic; we are inevitably concerned with right and wrong. "Is state enterprise or private enterprise more efficient?" is not the only relevant question; we must also know whether state enterprise is *better* or *worse* than private enterprise. For, while human values can be removed from scientific data without destroying the problem, they are an *integral* part of the social sciences: if human values are abstracted, the social sciences become irrelevant or worse.

Several further difficulties confront the social scientist. His subject does not lend itself to the experimental method of the physical scientist, who can isolate certain problems and set up experiments in which all conditions are kept constant except the ones he wants to observe. The social scientist cannot experiment; he must use such data as are available. The

social scientist may often change the data by the very process
of observation and publication of results. The classic example is that of the public-opinion polls. Once they know
what the general view is, many people will change their ideas
to conform with the majority—a few may also change in the
other direction.

In addition, the social scientist must deal with a problem
that is almost totally absent in the physical sciences. While
the theories of the physical scientist may be wrong, they will
seldom be *made* wrong by changes in the data. But the conditions the social scientist examines are constantly changing
and an insight that was valid in the past may no longer be
useful because of changes in conditions. For example, policies that might be appropriate in a newly developing country
would often be unnecessarily harsh in the same country once
it had attained a high standard of living.

Economics as it is taught in the vast majority of schools today exemplifies the failure of the social sciences to understand these major differences between the physical and social
sciences. Much of existing economic theory elevates the emotional preferences of Western society into immutable laws.
Its policy recommendations are usually achieved by using
simplified assumptions and ignoring the real world. It has
failed to adjust its theories to constantly changing conditions.
How did this come about? As economics developed in the
nineteenth century, it became concerned with the distribution of income—in particular it considered what forces determined the amount paid to labor, capital, and land. A sophisticated model was built up to prove that, *given a certain
set of assumptions,* the distribution of income achieved by
the free operation of market forces would be most efficient.
Ever since this model was completed, the main stream of economics has concentrated on working out its implications.

This theory is usually called neoclassical. However, the assumptions behind this theory, which include no government spending, no large firms, no unions, no change in technology, and complete awareness of new products and technologies, were never really fulfilled. It is necessary to recall only some of the developments that have taken place in the twentieth century to show how unrealistic these assumptions have now become. Government spending has increased rapidly and become a significant factor in the economies of all the rich countries. The large firm has become the norm. Unions have gained considerable power. One of the main ways in which the firm gains an advantage is by possessing more information than its competitors.

It might be suggested that Keynes's book, *The General Theory of Employment, Interest, and Money,* which was published in 1936 and which explained the mechanism by which slumps occurred, terminated the dominance of neoclassical thought. It is true that the Keynesian theory explaining the development of unemployment came to be accepted as correct, and that no economic textbook today could be written without discussing Keynesian ideas. However, the introduction of Keynesian theory has not led to the abandonment of neoclassical ideas, for neoclassical economics absorbed the Keynesian revolution. Unfortunately the resulting synthesis must necessarily be unsatisfactory, for the two theories are incompatible.

How can we explain the continued use of neoclassical theory when the irrelevance of its basic assumptions is recognized by most economists? The failure to modify the old theory stems in part from the formal beauty (the term is deliberately chosen) of the old economic model. The particular pattern of assumptions freed the economist from any need to worry about "human" attitudes. Within the model he had created trading took place mechanically on the basis of price; human beings carried out the transactions without affecting them in any significant way. A second reason for the continued use of the old theory has been the failure to develop a new economic theory more relevant to today's conditions. Economists have naturally been loath to accept that one body of theory was irrelevant as long as they had nothing to put in its place.

There is perhaps an even more fundamental reason. Neoclassical economic theory is based on and supports a doctrine that is deeply embedded in Western philosophy—that of the importance of the individual. It shows how each man seeking his own selfish interest—which is assumed to be monetary—will in some mysterious way bring about the common good. The destruction or abandonment of this theory would bring into question many of the ideas on which the private enterprise system is based.

We will find that the theory and set of principles of neoclassical economics are not valid in today's world. We will see that the proofs used by economists are based on inaccurate assumptions. The distribution of income achieved by the free operation of market forces is not necessarily best, government interference should not always be limited to a minimum, direct taxation is not always better than indirect, a balanced budget is not always the best policy, public and private costs and benefits do not inevitably coincide, free trade does not always maximize the value of production. The economic policy recommendations that stand—often unconsciously—behind much present action must be re-examined in the light of actual conditions.

We must develop a system of economic thought that values the relations between people, and takes account of the fact that much of the happiness in a person's life results from his contacts with others and from the existence of adequate community services. We will have to admit that while the increasing abundance of private goods has significantly eased the lives of many in the rich countries, the pattern of industry and trade necessary to allow this level of production often has side effects that reduce satisfaction. We will have to replace present unrealistic methods used to value the national income by a system that takes into account the whole life of each person in the community, rather than only "economic" factors as is the case at the present time.

One of the most important results of the acceptance of neoclassical economics was the stifling of debate on the "right" distribution of income. The particular set of assumptions adopted by economists made it possible to prove that the pattern of distribution of wealth that would be achieved by the operation of market forces would be "best." Thus the way in which the available resources should be divided among people was very little discussed for many decades and is still not considered a subject of major importance. We seldom seriously consider whether the highest rewards should be given to those with the greatest skill and education, who very often enjoy their work and would continue it even if their wages were lower, or whether the highest wages should be paid to compensate those who have the most unpleasant jobs. Economics is still relatively unwilling to study the implications of the fact that the wages received by the worker are no longer based solely on the value of the goods or services he produces, but also depend on the relative power of unions and management. Economics has not come to grips with the fact that the structure of wages and prices is heavily affected by past custom and that the effect of an increase in wages in one industry automatically sets up strong forces that tend to lead to increases in other areas of the economy. Its formal analysis is still largely limited to situations in which increases and decreases in wages and prices are determined by the supply and demand for goods rather than by relative bargaining power.

Economic theories about the automatic nature of the distribution of income through market forces require that it should be possible to identify the contribution of labor, capital, and land to any product. While this was theoretically reasonable when the worker had little aid from machinery, it is no longer realistic today. What, for example, is the contribution of a highly skilled technical worker in a large oil refinery? Without the technicians output would not be possible, with their services output is valued at millions of dollars—so how much should the technician be paid? Is the relevant criterion to make the job attractive enough to ensure that there will continue to be sufficient technicians? The problem goes deeper. The value of the output of the technician, and indeed of the refinery itself, depends upon the successful operation of the whole economy and society. It is only because society continues to exist that the output of the refinery has any value. A strike in any area of the economy now affects the income, health, and safety of those not immediately connected with the industry, through a myriad of direct and indirect effects. Each person has a value within the whole society; it could not function without him. The value of his services cannot therefore be assessed. This fact has long been recognized by economists in a more limited field. They have pointed out that if several workers co-operate closely in the manufacture of a specific product, the amount to be paid to each person is indeterminate. The line of reasoning above is therefore only an extension of one already accepted.

This is not the only argument that suggests that the right distribution of income is indeterminate. The Western countries are rich only because savings were made in the past and capital was invested, thus allowing larger production in later years. We have credited the shareholders with the saving and we have confined its benefits largely to them. But this saving was possible only because the standard of living of the greater part of the population was kept down. As we move into an economy of abundance, we have to decide who is entitled to the benefits of past saving.

The present theory of the stock market justifies the right of the shareholder to receive profits from the operation of industry. How relevant is this claim in today's conditions? The stock market grew out of the pattern of borrowing and lending in earlier centuries. At this period people bought shares in a particular enterprise they thought might be profitable. In many or most cases their participation was limited to a single trading venture. Upon its completion the profit from the venture was divided usually in proportion to the size of the initial stake—and the contract was thus terminated.

As the importance of manufacturing increased, the pattern changed. Money was committed for an indefinite period, there was no agreement that the enterprise would be dissolved at any specific date. Given the rapid change in wealth of the participants in the contract, this pattern soon raised considerable problems, for shareholders often wished to get their original investment back and use it for other purposes. This required that all the "partners" in the enterprise agreed on the terms of sale of the share—if agreement could not be reached, sale of the venture could be forced by one party to the contract. A further disadvantage was that each party was responsible for *all* the debts of the enterprise.

This system made the rapid extension of business difficult, for people were unwilling to commit funds to a number of ventures they could not keep under their own immediate control. While they might have been willing to risk a *fixed* sum in the success of a company, they would not put money into an enterprise—particularly a speculative one—if failure could force them to assume *all* the liabilities. The progress of the capitalist system depended, therefore, on the introduction of a method by which the liability of the shareholder was limited to the amount actually invested. If the firm were successful he could gain bountifully; if it failed he lost the money he had invested, but nothing more. This system of limited liability was introduced in the latter half of the nineteenth century. The spread of share ownership, however, required a further change. Given the semi-permanent nature of the enterprises in which people were now investing, it was essential that they should be able to sell their shares at the market price if they were in need of funds. Thus stock markets grew up to allow trading. Naturally, with the development of stock markets, trading was not limited to those in need of money; others took advantage of the situation to buy and sell shares in the hopes of choosing the most profitable.

As the concept of shareholding was originally an extension of the concept of partnership, it incorporated the idea that investors had the right to be consulted on decisions. In addition, it was held that they should receive their shares of the profits from the enterprise at regular intervals. The shareholders themselves were to decide on the best use of these distributed profits, reinvesting them in the company only if they felt that they wished to do so. Theory and practice started to diverge soon after the system was set up. The effective power of investors to control actions declined as their number increased. The right of the shareholders to decide whether profits should be reinvested in the firm or distributed diminished concurrently. The directors of the companies came to decide on the size of dividends, and their decisions were normally endorsed by the shareholders. It was accepted that a large proportion of the profit should be retained within the firm and used for expansion.

What then is the actual process on the stock market today and how does it compare with the theory that justifies the payment of dividends to those who provided capital? Neo-classical theory assumed that firms made large profits for only limited periods and that profits vanished as market forces brought the supply and demand for each particular type of goods into balance. Thus it was only the intelligent and far-sighted shareholder who obtained a large return on his investment, for only he was able to pick situations where the demand for particular goods was likely to be greater than the available supply and where profits were available.

Actual conditions are very different. Firms are able to control the prices of their goods so that they continue to make profits even if the demand for their goods is not very heavy. Several steel companies made profits in the latter half of 1960 although they were only producing at about 50 per cent of capacity. The firm is able to fix its prices for goods at such a level that the consumer not only pays for the labor and capital it took to produce the article he is buying but also contributes to the future expansion of the company. This ability of the firm to fix its prices at a level that will continue to allow profits leads to an increase in the value of the company and therefore in the value of each share: the holders of the shares benefit from this increase in value, as they are able to sell them at higher prices.

The effect of the stock market is therefore a peculiar one and one that is little understood: *it is actually the purchaser of goods who provides a large part of the funds required for the expansion of the firm.* The expansion of the firm increases the value of the company, the rising value of the company leads to an increase in the value of its shares, and this increase in the value of the shares accrues to their holders. But the customer who supplied the money for the expansion in the first place does not benefit from his contribution.

One further set of factors will force us to reconsider our methods of redistributing income. The validity of past economic theory depended upon its "proof," not only that everybody would receive his "just" share of production, but also that the economy would automatically be adjusted so that the demand for goods would always be equal to the supply; depressions were assumed to be impossible. Also, it was argued that the operation of the economy would assure that all those who wished to find work would be able to obtain it.

As we have seen, Keynes's new theory dealt the deathblow to this doctrine, although all its implications have not yet been accepted or indeed even analyzed. The basic point of his theory was that it was not necessarily true that the free operation of the economy would ensure that everybody could find a job. He demonstrated that a rising standard of living could often lead to depressions. People and firms would not want to spend all their money, but to save some of it; demand could then be insufficient to allow the purchase of all the goods that could be produced, firms would cut production because their unsold stocks would pile up, and this would lead to cuts in employment.

In coming years resources will be available to relieve poverty, to build schools, to construct roads, to accomplish slum clearance, to alter the distribution of wealth in favor of the poor. How are we to decide what we should do? Are the services of judges worth more or less than those of lawyers, educators, advertising men, and taxi drivers? We will have to decide how large a share of the available production should go to each citizen and we will have to decide on social rather than economic grounds. In the next chapter we will examine the operation of the mechanism that is believed to determine the distribution of wealth in the West.

# 4.

## Union-Management Bargaining: Conflict or Co-operation?

WESTERN COUNTRIES HAVE been willing to tolerate the inconvenience, damage, and sometimes even disaster that can be caused by strikes, because they have become convinced that the right to strike is basic to a democratic regime. It is fairly generally argued that the right to strike cannot be withdrawn without making negotiations meaningless and, indeed, destroying one of the essential bulwarks of freedom.

However, an increasing number of people are coming to believe that a system that allows a small group in a country to "blackmail" the other inhabitants cannot be wise or right. They point out that in the days when the strike weapon developed the two antagonists in the struggle were labor and management—the public was usually hardly affected. In pres-

ent conditions, however, the major strikes are often won or
lost because of their effect on the public. More time is therefore spent in trying to convince the public of the rights and
wrongs of the case so as to bring pressure to bear on the other
side than in hammering out a meaningful compromise between the parties. Criticisms of the system have so far failed
to make much headway because the social goals that the present system of negotiation between labor and management is
meant to achieve are considered more important than efficiency. This chapter examines whether the obvious economic
and social disadvantages of the system are, in fact, more than
counterbalanced by the freedom the system allows.

The confusion that is often manifested about the role of
unions and the fairly general suggestion that they are an
"ideal" institution is strange because they were developed to
counteract an evil rather than set up as being particularly
good in themselves. Early in the twentieth century it was recognized that the economic power of most manufacturers was
so much greater than that of each worker taken singly that
the laborer was unable to bargain for a fair wage. Labor unions were therefore given special rights far greater than those
allowed to other institutions, in the hope that this would lead
to a more equitable balance of power between industry and
labor. The unions have used this advantage skillfully and
have greatly improved the condition of the average worker.
But although the power disadvantage under which labor suffered in the past has diminished with changing social attitudes, the unions have not been prepared to give up their
favored position: they have wholeheartedly opposed any proposals to limit their present rights. It is therefore unrealistic
to claim that the present pattern of labor-management bargaining should necesarily be guarded inviolate, for this would
elevate a historical accident into an ideological necessity. We

must examine the effectiveness of the present system and discuss whether changes would improve it from the point of view of both labor and management and also from the point of view of society as a whole.

What is essential to meaningful labor-management bargaining? The first need is the existence of a permanent relationship between management and a body of workers represented by a union. The role of the union is to bargain with management and to obtain the highest wages and the widest possible range of benefits for the workers in the industry. The union is charged with the responsibility of improving wages and conditions of work in the *short run* and also with ensuring *lifetime* work for its members. In present conditions, however, the short- and long-run aims of unions are necessarily in direct and serious conflict. Unions are concerned to raise the income and improve the living standards of their members. But in so far as they are successful, they reduce employment for their members in the long run, for the increased cost of each worker will make it profitable to replace labor by machinery.

Developments in the steel industry can be used to illustrate the problems that may arise. Steelworkers have been obtaining large increases in wages since the end of World War II. Wages have risen some 15 per cent above those in the automobile industry: before the war the relationship was approximately the reverse. Indeed, wages in the steel industry have risen by greater percentages and greater absolute amounts than have those in almost any other industry. This rapid increase in wages made economical the major modernization program undertaken by the steel companies: the program was so successful that a 50-per-cent increase in production was possible with a practically unchanged labor force.

This is only one of the changes set in motion by the in-

crease in steel wages. The rapid increase in the price of steel
—prices rose some 70 per cent since 1947–48, compared to only
some 30 per cent for all industrial prices—weakened the competitive position of steel compared to other materials. New
products have been nibbling at markets that were previously
exclusively steel's. The amount of plastics used per car almost
doubled between 1954 and 1960; the use of aluminum in automobile production is expected to triple between 1960 and
1965. While some of these changes would probably have occurred in any case, they have been hastened and in some cases
initiated by the more rapid rise in steel prices compared to
those of other products. Imports of steel have also been encouraged and exports discouraged by the relatively high price.

The same development has occurred in other industries
where unions have been successful in raising wages rapidly
and have thus altered the price relation between one product
and another. Coal is a good example in both America and
Europe—the high price has forced many consuming industries to change to oil. Total employment in coal in America
has dropped to just over a quarter of the immediate postwar
level. Thus the greater the success of the labor unions in forcing up wages, the greater will tend to be the unfavorable
effect on long-run employment through the encouragement
of mechanization, the use of substitute materials, and the increase in imports. Unions are therefore confronted with an
intolerable dilemma: they must decide whether to give higher
priority to obtaining rapid increases in wages and fringe benefits for their workers, at the cost of decreasing the level of
employment in the industry, or to preserve jobs by limiting
wage claims. Unions have, of course, tried to obtain both advantages by demanding higher wages *and* job security, but
the pressure against "featherbedding" is undoubtedly increasing.

It is fair to say that not all the unions have been aware of the full implications of the dilemma. The mineworkers have pushed up wages so fast they have caused major unemployment problems: in many areas there are no alternative employment possibilities, and some old mining areas are classified as depressed. In so far as unions have understood the problem, they have still tended to pay more—if not exclusive—attention to immediate wage increases and other benefits, leaving the resulting fall in employment to the future.

This situation is now changing. Three items of labor news that appeared on the front page of the New York *Times* of October 20, 1960, will demonstrate the very divergent solutions that are being developed. A legal decision held that a union-management agreement limited or prohibited a clothing manufacturer from moving his plant from a relatively high-wage unionized area to a lower-wage area in the South. A second development was the announcement of an industrywide plan that provides severance benefits for workers in the International Ladies Garment Workers Union whose employers go out of business. On the West Coast an agreement was reached between dockers and management that did away with much featherbedding in an industry that had been long notorious for it. The agreement guaranteed the longshoremen against any major decline in their earnings following this change.

Although changes of this type would partially protect the worker from the unfavorable effects of wage increases, it remains true that the conflict between long- and short-run goals must gravely hamper the trade unions. The right solution to this dilemma can be developed only after we have understood what labor-management bargaining is meant to achieve and what it actually does. The main claim is that it alters the income received by labor and management and that the result-

ant changes will be good for the economy. This theory that
labor-management bargaining can influence relative incomes
depends essentially on theories derived from neoclassical economics. It was argued in this economic model that the market
forces of supply and demand determined the price that could
be charged for goods: given this determinacy of prices, any
increase in wages would necessarily cut into profits. This theory, however, is irrelevant today, for management does not
allow market forces to set its prices, but determines them primarily on the basis of the cost of production plus a margin
for profit. Under these circumstances an increase in wage
costs is usually followed by an increase in selling prices and
little change in the relation between wages and profits. It is,
however, true that only the large firm has this power to any
important extent.

Daniel Bell clarified the implications of this pattern for the
large company in an article in *Commentary* in March 1960:
"The point of all this (to return to the role of collective bargaining) is that the net effect of union pressure—apart from
the gains which have been won for the small group of highly
organized workers—has been to help install a mechanism
whereby the large corporation is able to strengthen its price
position in the market. In the past, price protection was
achieved by "basing point" systems (now outlawed), price
umbrellas (in which U.S. Steel took the lead), or informal
collusion. Today the union serves as the vehicle. (According
to Walter Reuther, for *every* dollar of increased labor costs
since 1947, General Motors by 1956 imposed about $3.75 in
cumulative price increases on the American car buyer. In
effect, the United Auto Workers, taking a small share of the
increased profits, has become, albeit unwillingly, the "junior
partner" of General Motors.) The companies can truthfully
say that they do not like the union negotiations, since other

than wage demands are often involved (work rules, fringe benefits, etc.). And the companies are usually inclined to resist the union's demands strenuously. But it invariably turns out that union negotiation offers a lovely opportunity to increase prices . . ." Thus labor-management bargaining tended to result primarily in higher prices for the consumer while the relative position of worker and shareholder remained more or less unchanged. As we saw in the previous chapter, this pattern ensures that the consumer provides much of the funds for the expansion of the firm.

If this is the pattern of labor-management bargaining, can we assume that its effects on the distribution of income between classes and individuals will be really satisfactory? In the years immediately after the war the powerful unions were most successful in forcing large increases in their wages and thus obtained more than a proportionate share of the increase in the national income. Their success distributed income away from workers with weaker unions, from the non-unionized worker as well as from the middle class and those with fixed incomes. It did not take long, however, for the other unions to understand the effects of this process and they were soon using the stronger unions as pace setters in their demands for increased wages. In the 1950's, therefore, unionized labor—and management whose salary increases were pushed upward *pari-passu* with union gains—tended to obtain the largest share of the increase in national income at the expense of the non-unionized worker and those with fixed incomes. This result was achieved partly by a more rapid rise in the incomes of unionized labor, and partly by the effects of inflation, which reduced the value of many forms of savings.

During the 1950's it was slowly recognized that the existing pattern of labor-management bargaining gave a fundamental advantage to those represented by strong unions. Those who had retired, who worked in such fields as government, community service, or education, as well as the unorganized worker, did not receive their fair share of the increase in resources that occurred in America. Pressures have therefore built up demanding that all those who have been left behind in the past decade receive a fair share of the increase in income to be expected in the 1960's. For example, it was the dissatisfaction of the old with their position that made the medical-health bill a major issue in the 1960 election. It was the failure of minimum wages to rise along with the national income that caused President Kennedy to put forward as one of his first legislative proposals an increase in the minimum wage. It is the inability of many educational institutions to pay decent salaries to their teachers, which has caused many politicians to back a program of government aid for this purpose.

It will no longer be possible to allow the benefits from a rising national income to be distributed so that those with most economic power benefit to the largest extent and others are virtually excluded. Steps will inevitably be taken to aid those most in need of additional goods—the underpaid unorganized worker and the older person who earned his living when wages were lower and when incomes were too small to allow large saving or whose savings were destroyed by the great depression of the thirties or halved by postwar inflation. The standard of living we enjoy today is the result of the effort of past generations—without their work we would not be able to achieve the present unparalleled rate of increase in production (about $25 billion per year at the beginning of the sixties and $40 billion at the end of the sixties). It is elementary justice that the old should benefit from the higher standards now available rather than try to live on incomes that were standard when the country was poorer.

Some European and American pension schemes are based on the idea that those who have retired should receive a set proportion of the actual level of income in the profession or industry. Thus, when wages or salaries are raised for existing workers, the retired also benefit. This system is used on the French railway system. It has also been standard practice, until recently, for retired military personnel in the United States. In the same way, government pensions should be based, not on the amount that each person paid into the scheme, but on a proportion of the average income in the country at the time the pension is being paid.

Our present methods of labor-management bargaining, therefore, do not result in the "right" division of income among the various classes in society and among various industries. We must look for new ideas that will allow greater justice. The interests of labor and management are no longer clear-cut, nor do they necessarily correspond to those of society. There is an ancient conflict between management and labor—management must be interested in keeping its costs down while labor must be interested in raising wages. There is a basic conflict between the traditional short-run interests of the union—a rise in wages and other benefits—and their long-term interest in the preservation of employment. There is a conflict between the interests of labor, in pre-empting the benefits of an increase in production, and that of society as a whole, requiring that the rise in income should be distributed more equitably. There may be a conflict in the future between management's desire to reduce employment, in order to keep costs down, and the existing requirement that jobs should be available for all.

The conventional wisdom poses the basic issue in labor-management bargaining in terms of wages and conditions in a single industry: in actual fact negotiations eventually in-

volve the whole economy. Decisions made in one industry affect others directly and through a hundred indirect routes.
The frustration that has developed through the misunderstanding of the actual forces affecting labor-management bargaining—each side feels that the other is acting unreasonably
—has led to a definite worsening of labor-management relations in the last couple of years. Despite the payment of record wages in all sectors of the economy—and payment at levels
that would have been considered inconceivable only twenty
years ago—many lengthy strikes have occurred and others
have been avoided only by continuing government pressure.
Conditions have changed so rapidly that neither management
nor labor is clear about the extent of its prerogatives and the
demands each is entitled to make or refuse. For example, it is
generally agreed that the record length of the 1959 steel strike
resulted, not from the clash over wage rates, but from management's demand for the right to change conditions of work.
This latter demand rallied labor's forces when the refusal of
a demand for higher wages had failed to do so. Labor was
prepared to strike to preserve its rights, but appeared unwilling to do so in order to gain greater benefits.

A few companies have recognized this breakdown in the
labor-management bargaining process and have done their
best to move into the gap by unilaterally developing a new
philosophy. They argue that the company itself should weigh
the claims of the worker against those of the shareholder and
the consumer and decide how much the worker is entitled to
receive. Within such a philosophy the union has little place;
its role is conceptualized as merely helping the company in
deciding on the proper benefits. The union, however, still
feels that it should be an independent bargaining agent; it
will almost inevitably ask for more than the company feels is
justified.

In 1960 the International Union of Electrical Workers struck against General Electric. The stated reason was a disagreement about proposed contract terms, but these were actually relatively unimportant. The strike was really to decide if G.E. was to make the decisions, with the I.U.E. acting as a mere provider of information for the management of the company, or if it was to *negotiate* with the I.U.E.—G.E. representing the interests of management and the I.U.E. representing the interests of labor. Because of its ideological overtones the strike generated considerable bitterness, particularly among the leaders of the union. However, they had only lukewarm support from many of the workers they represented, who believed that G.E.'s offer was adequate, and the strike was therefore settled on the terms offered by G.E. *before* the strike started.

A very important question is raised by the failure of this strike and its probable effects on the future pattern of union-management bargaining. Can we allow management to make its own decisions without intervention from other forces, or should workers be able to draw support from other sources? We have to ask and answer new questions. We need to consider whether the old policies of the unions, which were devised in an age when the first concern of all employers was their own interests and those of the shareholders, are adequate today when the doctrine of social responsibility is more generally accepted. We must examine whether a company, however benevolent, should be the only power to control the life of its workers and the rewards to which they are entitled. We need to consider the mechanisms that can be set up on a national scale to determine the "right" distribution of national income without inhibiting the possibilities of local adjustment.

Our discussions about the right patterns to adopt must be

heavily affected by the fact that our present economic system contains the elements of a fundamental conflict between the interests of producers and those of the society as a whole. We have seen that, despite the rapid increase in the production of goods, the number of people employed to produce them has been declining. In the years since the war this has not led to a crisis, for the rate of increase in the labor force has been relatively small and there has been an increased demand for labor in the service sectors—particularly in selling and office work. Machines are now being developed that will decrease the demand for labor in both these fields. In addition, the total labor force will increase more rapidly in future years, for it will be swollen by the increased birth rate. The amount of goods that *can* be produced will rise, but unless we make deliberate policy decisions there can be no certainty that people will have enough money to enable them to buy the goods that can be produced. We return to this problem in Chapter 7.

It would seem that we must develop new methods that will allow a more satisfactory distribution of income. But, to do this, we must change our attitudes, for it is now considered unnecessary to develop a "theory" about the right distribution of income: it is claimed that such decisions should be left to "free market forces," that is to say, labor-management bargaining. We have always assumed that the gap between the income levels of various classes and types of individuals is necessary if growth is to be ensured. In a world where an adequate income can be assured for all this reasoning is no longer fully applicable. We must therefore decide on the basis of value judgments how much greater the income of a corporation president should be than that of his workers; how much more or less the garbage man should earn because his job is unpleasant. We can no longer assume that these social decisions are pre-empted by economic imperatives.

Society must determine what degree of inequality of income it considers justified, and then decide what types of jobs should receive the highest incomes. In the past the skills required for professional work have received a large reward because of their scarcity: those doing the most unpleasant jobs have obtained the lowest incomes because a large proportion of the population has been able to do only this type of work. The professional and technical worker is often highly paid for doing things he enjoys: the garbage man is paid a low wage for work he would wish to avoid. Can this situation be allowed to continue?

This is only part of the problem. The basic issue is to decide on the limits of responsibility that each society has to all its members. Until quite recent years we have assumed that each person should earn enough money to support himself and his family and to cover disasters such as long illnesses and other major setbacks. More recently the governments of many Western countries have decided to help people when they need assistance, but often on terms that make it clear that the individual has failed and is being helped only because of the "generosity" of the state. We have been economically justified in distributing resources on the basis of success and failure in economic competition in the past: in the future we must decide whether it is morally right to distribute resources on this basis in an economy of abundance.

A "moral" policy would not have been possible in the past, for it was essential that everybody be forced to work. Today this imperative no longer applies; indeed consideration of trends in productivity suggests that the preservation of full employment may be very difficult in coming decades. We have to examine how far the government should moderate the forces of economic competition. We must decide what guarantees we should give to all the members of a society of abundance. The next two chapters study how much government intervention is necessary in such a society, and discuss the ways in which public actions should be financed.

# 5.

## The Responsibilities of Government

THE MANAGEMENT-UNION bargaining process does not only change the wage structure within a particular industry; it also affects the distribution of income throughout the society. However, government activities are equally important in determining the distribution of wealth. It may be helpful to list just a few of the ways in which government actions change the amount of income available to various classes and groupings of society: types of goods purchased by government; activities subsidized by the government and those it taxes; the levels of direct taxation and methods the individual can legally use to reduce his tax burden; what are the size and duration of unemployment benefits; how large are welfare benefits to those unable to support themselves and on what conditions are they made available.

Many people do not want to concede that the effect of government actions *must* be examined when the distribution of income is being considered. They argue that government actions should not be *allowed* to interfere with market forces. The opponents of government intervention rely on two different lines of argument: one economic and one political. The economic argument is based once again on the incomplete and inaccurate assumptions of neoclassical theory, which "proved" that the distribution of income would necessarily be most efficient if it were determined entirely by market forces.

The political theory that demands the limitation of government action is based on utilitarianism: on the belief that the "selfish" action of the individual will necessarily result in the greatest good of the greatest number. If this theory is true, it follows that the government should not intervene in the economy, for any change would be for the worse as it would interfere with the freedom of action of individuals. Whatever the validity of this theory in the nineteenth century, it has little relevance in the twentieth. Few people can make their own particular interests known at the present time; they must act through a collective, whether it be the AFL-CIO association of labor unions; the National Association of Manufacturers; a consumers' organization; or a welfare group. None of these groupings will reflect exactly the desires of the individual—indeed they will normally afford a very imperfect picture of his over-all wishes.

This banding together of people so that they can express their *common* interests produces a new facet to an old problem: the use of power. Some groups will be particularly effective in influencing the government to establish the policies they want; others will have less success. Associations of manufacturers or labor unions are probably at one end of the scale of effectiveness; at the other may lie organizations representing the interests of consumers. If government merely reflects the pressure each group can bring to bear, the interests of the best-organized and strongest groups will obtain most attention, and those of weaker groups will be neglected. Government must therefore do more than merely arbitrate between the interests of conflicting groups if it is to maximize the welfare of its citizens.

We sometimes *contrast* the interests of government with those of the individual. But the government should not be antipathetic to the people; it should reflect their wishes. The real question we should consider is whether certain types of activity can be more successfully carried out by the joint action of the community or by the separate individuals or interests within it. It is now commonly agreed that such functions as building and maintaining roads, providing an adequate police force, and ensuring safe sanitation and water supplies fall within the purview of government. But the adoption of many functions by government is recent, and we cannot therefore freeze the list of proper activities as it exists today: we must be willing to continue to re-examine the division between the efforts of the private person and institution and those of the government. Only historical accident can explain why sewage and water are almost always public responsibilities, while gas and electricity are often provided by private enterprise in the United States. In other Western countries the line between government activity and private enterprise is drawn differently. We must re-examine the situation as it is today if we are to produce an adequate division of responsibilities in changing circumstances. We will return to the political problem this raises in Chapter 9.

We can now discuss the economic reasoning advanced to prove that the government should limit its actions to a minimum. As some government action is now obviously necessary and generally accepted, the argument against government activity has been transmuted into a claim that the effect of government intervention on the economy should be "neutral," that it should not benefit one group as compared to another. For example, in a report published in 1960, entitled "Federal Transportation Policy and Program," it was suggested that "the transportation system should be regulated by the same forces as the rest of the American free enterprise system: fair competition in price and service to the customers . . . conditions in the transportation industries, once a larger degree of market and cost information become available, promise workable results under substantially reduced regulation."

This proposal for a "neutral" pattern is unrealistic: both because such a policy would be impossible to devise and carry out and also because it would not be economically satisfactory. We can best examine the implications of any such attempt in the field of transportation. In order to attain this goal a major revolution would have to occur in pricing policies, and appropriate charges would have to be made for facilities that are now given free or below cost—roads, canals, and airport services. The tax burdens on the railroads would have to be limited or those on road transport increased. It is doubtful if any really satisfactory scale of charges could be devised, and even if this were possible any attempt to adopt such charges would raise considerable, if not insoluble, political difficulties. However, even these changes would not be sufficient to guarantee a neutral transportation policy.

Two other sets of conditions would have to be satisfied to attain government neutrality among types of transportation. First, access to government funds for each type of transportation would have to be equally easy or difficult. Second, the government programs of research and development would have to be arranged in such a way that they would not give one form of transportation an advantage over others. We can see how far we are away from the first of these conditions when we contrast the attention given to the road and air programs in America with the neglect of the railroads. The fact that the government takes over the responsibility for finding money to create and preserve the facilities needed by one type of transportation while taxing others heavily makes neutrality an unreal concept.

Theoretically the system could be changed to avoid this result. But there is no way of overcoming the further bar to neutrality that arises from the fact that the government must help some forms of transportation by its research expenditures and fail to advance others. We can use the example of the relative progress of the aircraft manufacturers and the railroads in recent years as an example. The airlines have moved through several generations of aircraft in this time and are now flying jet planes near the speed of sound—they expect to fly jet planes at twice the speed of sound by 1970. The railroads, on the other hand, have made practically no progress toward higher speeds. While many factors have combined to produce this result—notably the dynamism of aircraft management and the inertia of the railroads—the major factor in the differing rates of progress has been the amount of government money poured into aircraft research compared with its absence on the railroads. The problem of producing a 200-m.p.h. fixed-rail method of transport is almost certainly less difficult and more urgent than that of producing a supersonic passenger jet, but the fact that military research is required for aircraft and missiles and is not carried out on railroad problems makes it probable that the second will be achieved before the first. This bias is irremediable, given the present state of the cold war.

Still further sources of bias exist in the field of transporta-

tion. One is the division between private and public ownership. Once an automobile has been purchased, the owner's
choice of methods of transport is always heavily in its favor.
He must pay the costs of depreciation, garaging, etc., whether
he uses his car or not. When he determines the cost of a trip
in his car, he should rationally take account *only* of the additional costs of running his automobile—gas and oil consumption and additional repairs. On the other hand, airplane, bus,
and rail companies must cover in the price of their tickets
not only the running cost of their equipment but also charges
for depreciation, fixed facilities, etc. Although the *total* cost
per passenger of running a car is often higher than the *total*
cost per passenger of running communal forms of transportation, the actual out-of-pocket cost to the car user is often
lower. If the additional convenience of using a car is considered—particularly in today's conditions, when public transport has often become unsatisfactory—it is not surprising that
automobiles are very often the preferred form of transportation.

In many countries, however, the private convenience of using a car may be outweighed by the social cost and inconvenience it causes. The automobile was developed as a means of
mass transportation in the United States. The vast distances
and the comparatively limited population density made it a
particularly appropriate method of moving people. However,
even in America the continuing growth of metropolitan areas
is challenging the continued expansion of automobile use. In
many parts of the country the excess of cars compared to
available roads is destroying the very advantages the automobile is meant to provide. Even in Los Angeles, which developed from the start as a city planned for automobiles, it has
proved impossible to provide freeways fast enough to allow
for the increase in traffic—Los Angeles is now considering the

construction of some type of rapid transport system.

The pattern of automobile use that was built up in America is now being allowed to develop in other parts of the world. However, when we examine the difference in conditions in America and Europe, it becomes obvious that Europe cannot afford to base her whole system of transportation on the American pattern. Population densities are so much greater that sufficient space could not be given over to roads. Nevertheless, Europe appears to be content to try to imitate the American system and to allow people to buy cars until they choke the roads. This policy is based largely on an unwillingness to tamper with the free choice of the citizen as to how he wants to spend his money: this unwillingness stems in turn from the fact that a theory has not yet been developed to prove that problems of road congestion may sometimes be insoluble—that certain intensities of car use cannot be accommodated without destroying the area they are meant to serve. Problems of traffic congestion have generally been approached from the point of view of the traffic engineer. New roads have been constructed, important road junctions widened, bottlenecks eliminated. People have been disappointed when these techniques have not been successful in eliminating traffic congestion even at the points that have been improved, and when the situation has continued to deteriorate in all other areas where improvements have not been carried out.

London Transport (the public transport system in London, England) has put forward a theory that would account for the failure of engineering works to improve the situation. They point out that normally decisions as to whether to use a car, employ other means of transportation, or even travel at all depend in large part on the degree of congestion. If the amount of time spent in driving or the nervous irritation becomes too great because of delays and dangerous conditions, people will eventually decide to switch to other forms of transportation or will avoid traveling. Their travel will be "frustrated." When new roads are constructed or other improvements made, those who had given up driving will reexamine whether it has become worth while to use their cars again. Others will take advantage of the improved conditions to reroute their journeys. As a result, the effect of the changes is swamped by the increase in car use. The relevance of this theory can be demonstrated by the continuing failure to forecast the increase in traffic volume in Los Angeles—new freeways have been jammed within months of their completion rather than after the period of years originally forecast.

There is now "frustrated traffic" in most of the major cities of the world and in a large number of metropolitan areas. Any feasible program of construction of roads and parking areas cannot solve the problem. Traffic congestion can be reduced to tolerable levels only by some program that would limit the number of people who wish, or are allowed, to use the roads. One method of achieving this end would be to use the price mechanism, forcing people to pay the full value of the road space they occupy. Another possibility would be to limit driving privileges to certain groups: such as doctors.

No program for limiting the use of roads to certain people has ever been worked out except under the most compelling conditions. Admittedly the taxes levied on the purchase and use of cars in several European countries and even in America are high, but the justification for these taxes is hardly ever in terms of their favorable effect on the level of road congestion but in terms of the amount of revenue they will raise for government operations. Similarly, the limitation of parking rights in certain cities has been carried out on an *ad hoc* basis, with the responsibility for the justification of measures resting with those who would introduce the restrictions.

The problem of introducing any rational program of automobile use in the United States is gravely increased by the fact that most American cities now have inadequate or almost nonexistent public transport facilities. Any policy limiting the right to use an automobile would have to be accompanied by a revolutionary change in the quantity and quality of public transportation. The technical means of providing adequate public transportation are already available or shortly will be: moving pavements, individual subway cars, possibly self-driven taxis. But the attitudes needed for their adoption are still missing. For example, New York still finds itself unable to afford the funds to build an additional subway in 1961, although it built several at the beginning of the century, when its resources were far smaller.

One final problem raised by the whole pattern of the industrial society can be mentioned here. We have developed a system of industrial "efficiency"—where a man at his job is considered part of a productive system and is expected to work as part of this system. Within this area of his life man is expected to be "efficient" and the productivity of his work and that of the machines he controls is carefully calculated. The rest of his time, however, is passed at "leisure": he is then little concerned with efficiency. One of the most-discussed problems in public transportation is that much equipment is used only four hours a day: we see little discussion of the fact that private cars are often used for less than an hour a day. We will return to other implications of this attitude in Chapter 10.

Essential government action will *inevitably* affect the costs and benefits in the field of transportation; however, this is not the only area in which government intervention is necessary. It may be useful to discuss briefly one further area where government intervention is still not fully accepted: the preservation and validation of resources. We still give little attention to one of the most vital problems for the continuation of life on this planet. Almost generally throughout the world water is being used faster than reserves are being replenished. An article in *Harper's Magazine*, by Robert and Liona Rienow, came to a conclusion that is typical for observers in this field:

"There is only one way to avoid a water crisis in the coming years: a national water policy carried out on all levels of government and including new measures of reforestation and conservation. We must slow down that part of the water cycle between the cloud and the sea, during which water is available to us. We must regulate our water use instead of merely supplying water to all and sundry on a catch-as-catch-can basis."

The sensible application of economic theories in this area would help to reduce wastage. Because the availability of water has raised no problem until recent years, excessive use has been generally condoned. If water is scarce, however, it must be treated as valuable and its price should be adjusted to reflect its scarcity. That this could have an important effect is shown by the experience of one steel mill located in an area where water is in short supply—this mill manages to produce steel using about 2 per cent of the amount of water per ton of steel found necessary for production in other areas.

Similar problems arise in the case of many raw materials. The resulting situation was documented in the Paley report —a United States Government survey studying existing raw material use and future prospects. Although the report was published in 1950, its conclusions are still relevant. The report showed how raw material use in the United States had increased over the previous half century. "By 1950—in comparison with the year 1900—we were taking from the earth: two and one-half times more bituminous coal; three times more copper; three and one-half times more iron-ore; four times more zinc; twenty-six times more natural gas; thirty times more crude oil."

In terms of absolute quantities this meant that "At mid-century, over 2½ billion tons of materials are being used up each year to keep the country going and support its high standard of living . . . each person uses up, on an average, some 18 tons a year. He uses about 14,000 pounds of fuel for heat and energy. . . . He uses 10,000 pounds of building materials . . . plus 800 pounds of metals winnowed from 5,000 pounds of ores. He eats nearly 1,600 pounds of food; this together with cotton and other fibers for clothing, pulpwood for paper and other miscellaneous products mounts up to 5,700 pounds of agricultural products. In addition, he uses 800 pounds of nonmetalics, such as lime, fertilizer, and chemical raw materials."

The policies of the American Government continue, however, to be largely based on the earlier ideas that America's reserves of raw materials are inexhaustible. The money spent by government in this field usually encourages practices that will lead to earlier discovery and use rather than conservation. The danger of these actions is shown by the fact that production of petroleum in 1950 represented 8 per cent of known reserves, that of lead represented 6 per cent, that of iron ore 5.9 per cent, that of zinc 3.8 per cent, and that of copper 3.6 per cent.

It is particularly important to beware of naïveté when studying the need for conservation. There is little doubt that, given the pace and intensity of research expenditures today, substitutes can be found for materials that become scarce. We already know that within a few years it will be possible to obtain fresh water from the ocean at a "reasonable" cost; we are informed that when the rich ores are exhausted we will be able to extract metals from low-grade ores or even from igneous rocks. But these changes will be costly; it will be far more expensive to extract metals from low-grade ores. We need to develop a conservationist attitude to resources, to use as little as possible rather than as much as possible.

Conservation is necessary for another reason. Even if it is accepted that sea water can be made fresh and minerals can be extracted from very low-grade ores, this will be possible only in a society where social co-operation has reached a very high level. For in these conditions the failure of one group in society to perform its role would totally disrupt the economy. Not even the most optimistic would suggest that we have reached a state where we can rely on the acceptance of social responsibility by all, nor does it seem likely that we will reach it within a period of years or even decades. We cannot yet move over to such a complex system.

In today's interrelated world the interests of the individual and the community as a whole do not necessarily coincide. The community should not tolerate slums; the individual may not be able to do much about them and may even profit from their continuance. The community as a whole will benefit from an adequate education system; the individual cannot always afford to pay to complete his studies. The selfish actions of the individual or the private firm, the labor union and the co-operative will not necessarily maximize the satisfaction of all. The whole community, acting through its government, must influence and control the evolution of the economy and society. In order to perform this task it must have access to adequate funds. Present methods will not be adequate to raise the required money: new policies will have to be developed.

# 6.

## *Financing Government Activities*

A GOVERNMENT CAN USE three different methods to obtain the funds it requires to meet its obligations. First, it can tax its citizens and institutions, thus gaining possession of their money. Second, it can borrow money from people and institutions and pay interest on the amount it borrows. Third, it can simply create money and use the resulting funds to make its purchases. The first part of this chapter will be concerned with the assumptions that cause one method of raising funds to be preferred to another: the second part with changes in taxation policy that would be favorable.

The way in which money should be raised depends on the relation between supply and demand in the economy. Nineteenth-century economic theory assumed that the supply of goods and the demand for them would *always* and *necessarily* be in balance. It followed logically that if the government wished to buy more goods it should do so only after it had arranged for a decrease in the amount of goods bought by its citizens and its institutions, for otherwise there would be more money to buy goods than products available for purchase. Two methods of transferring funds to the government were considered appropriate. Money for use in non-investment expenditures—education, police, welfare payments, etc. —was to be obtained by taxation. Money for investment was sometimes to be obtained by taxation, but it was also sometimes considered justifiable to borrow.

The one point on which everybody agreed before 1936 was that the government should never simply create funds. The prohibition against creating funds was based on the assumption that the demand for goods would always be equal to supply as long as government did not interfere with the economy. Keynes destroyed the validity of this assumption when he showed that there was no certainty that the demand for goods would always be equal to the available supply in the rich countries. Almost entirely because of his theoretical analysis a change has taken place in the accepted budgetary policy. It is now generally agreed that it is justifiable for the government to spend more money during a slump than it receives from taxation and borrowing, i.e., to run a budget deficit. But this change in recommended policy is still fairly limited; many believe that any extra debt incurred in a recession should be paid back during boom periods. This proposal, however, may be unreasonable. It seems possible that, with progress toward an abundant society, private demand may become insufficient to absorb the potential supply and that government should create funds to fill the gap. Such a statement seems shocking to some: they would argue that the creation of funds by the government will necessarily be inflationary, and in addition will deprive the private firm and private persons of funds they could use. But this reasoning is purely conventional, for if we changed our values it could easily seem appropriate for the government to take over a function now performed by the banks—that of the creation of funds.

The Western economy runs on credit. We willingly concede the right of the producer and the consumer to use credit, but we deny this right to government. Our views in this field come from the past conventional wisdom: they are not relevant in present conditions. We should not forget that only a relatively few years ago the wisdom and the ethics of allowing the consumer to go into debt were almost as hotly disputed as the question of whether the government should be allowed to go further into debt is today.

Given the present system of economic organization in Western countries at the present time, the major problem is to ensure that the demand for goods stays equal to the potential supply. There was a period during the 1930's when it was thought that the problem of keeping demand equal to supply would prove insoluble. However, postwar experience in this field has been relatively favorable up to the present time. Why have the Western countries been more successful in this task in postwar years than in the 1930's? The relatively favorable position is due in part to the revolution in the desired standard of living that has taken place in the last fifteen years. It also results from the high level of military spending. Perhaps the main cause, however, has been an alteration in the distribution of income.

This last point should be developed. The demand for goods depends not only upon *total* income but also upon the *distribution* of income. In 1929 the upper 1 per cent of the nation's family units in America (i.e., families or individuals) got 19 per cent of the nation's disposable income. By 1948 this percentage had shrunk to less than 9 per cent. If this change had not taken place, it is certain that we would now be suffering from the most drastic slump ever experienced, for the top 1 per cent of income receivers would have failed to spend a large part of their income and the demand for goods would have been completely unequal to the potential supply. On the other hand, if the national income were to be distributed with absolute equality, everybody would attempt to spend most of his income, total savings would shrink to a very low level, and the demand for goods would exceed supply. One of the ways in which the economy of the *rich* countries can be kept in balance is by altering the distribution of income in favor of the poor members of society.

There are other methods that could be used to close any gap between supply and demand. It would be possible to decrease the level of supply without greatly affecting demand by cutting hours of work and leaving wages unchanged. It would be possible to raise the desire for goods by making people feel that more products were necessary for the good life and a decent standard of living. The government could simply take up the slack between actual and potential production by building new schools, by demolishing slum housing and building new accommodation, and by controlling pollution. Because there would be unused resources in the economy, the government would not need to raise this money by taxation or by borrowing, the money could simply be created. The additional funds would not cause inflation, for there is—by definition—no shortage of goods.

This raises new problems. Historically there has always been a shortage of goods, and the controlling factor in the rate of growth has been the amount of *saving* and *investment;* today in America it is the *effective demand* for goods that is the factor determining the rate of growth. The traditional line of reasoning was that we should encourage firms to invest additional funds and thus increase plant capacity. It was claimed that this additional capacity would lead to the production of additional goods. Today this reasoning does not apply. America has both the productive capacity *and* the unemployed labor that would allow it to produce additional goods. It is the lack of demand for these goods that prevents the economy from expanding. If we allow additional demand to develop, we would call forth the necessary supply and increase both total income and income per head.

The lesson we must learn is that in a society of abundance deliberate policy actions will be required to make sure that effective demand is sufficient to allow the purchase of all the goods that can be supplied. The government can balance supply and demand in many ways—one possibility is to run a budget deficit, spending more than is received in taxes. While this possibility is actually reasonable and realistic, it could not be applied at the present time. A large budget deficit is *believed* to be evidence of irresponsible government policy and will be treated as such: thus foreign banks and other institutions will react as though the budget deficit were irresponsible. Only when it is recognized that budget deficits may be appropriate in a society of abundance will they be feasible.

For this reason taxation will remain the chief source of government funds for many years. The remainder of this chapter is devoted to discussing the danger of a breakdown in the present taxation systems in the West and the immediate solutions that might be applied. The basic fact that must be remembered is the large percentage of income now taken in taxes in almost all the rich countries of the world—in the United States 25 per cent of the national income, in France about 31 per cent, in West Germany about 35 per cent. During the decade 1950–60, U.S. federal taxes rose by about 130 per cent, state taxes about 110 per cent, and local taxes about 135 per cent. The debt burden of state and local authorities in the United States has increased at dramatic speed; federal indebtedness has increased only slightly. There can be no doubt that the increase in total government expenditures—federal, state, and local—from $55 billion in 1950 to an estimated $125 billion in 1960 has gravely strained present taxation methods. It is often suggested by observers that we should reduce the tax burden to its earlier level and allow private initiative to take over once more. This solution is inadequate to present needs, for as we saw in the previous chapter, many tasks could be adequately carried out only by government authorities. We must expect the rise in government spending to continue.

It would seem that the sums needed for community services could be raised with less difficulty if different methods of taxation were adopted. We often make the mistake of assuming that the techniques now employed are part of a "system" of taxation. In actual fact they grew haphazardly under the influence of economic theory, political necessities and possibilities, and historical accident. The tax most commonly used throughout the world and the one found most acceptable by economists is the income tax. It was first introduced in the middle of the nineteenth century, but it had little importance until the beginning of the twentieth. Its first use in the United States (apart from a brief period during and after the Civil War) occurred in 1913, after a constitutional amendment had been passed to make direct taxes legal. Income tax receipts now account for around half of central government revenue in many of the richer countries of the world, and it is the major instrument used to try to force the rich citizens to pay a larger share of taxes than the poor.

The second major source of federal taxes in America is the corporation tax. This developed conceptually from the tax on private incomes, and theories about its effects still often parallel those devised to explain the operation of the personal income tax. Other taxes used by central governments include sales and excise taxes and different forms of payroll taxes—these last are often earmarked to pay unemployment and social security benefits.

Property taxes (on the value of land and buildings) still provide the major source of revenue for local authorities, but their relative importance in the United States has decreased rapidly in recent years. These taxes raised only 59 per cent of all local taxes in 1959, compared to 87 per cent a decade ago. Sales taxes have probably been the major new source of revenue during this period, over 1500 local sales taxes now exist in the nation.

The threefold split in responsibilities that exists in the United States in federal, state, and local jurisdictions, coupled with the fact that only in recent years have state expenditures risen rapidly, has left state authorities with a basically unsatisfactory tax position. They rely on a large number of different taxes, none of which is really adequate—property taxes, sales taxes, gasoline taxes, license charges, income taxes, corporation taxes, and many others. Their efforts to raise funds for state operations are made more difficult by the fact that a high level of state taxation can drive much-needed industries out of the state and cause them to relocate in others where the tax burden is lighter.

The extent of the rise in taxation and the consequent strain have not yet been fully recognized. It still comes as a shock to see statistics such as those given in an article on the whole suburban tax situation, published in September 1959 by the New York *Times:* "At present the average suburban taxpayer is 29 years old and has a wife, two children and often his own house. He earns $5,183 a year and is giving ten years of his lifetime wages to taxes. At current levels his lifetime taxes will be $20,870 on income, $7,710 on real property and the rest in other levies." In the same report Professor Robert Wood said: "I see a revolt coming in the United States on taxes and services. We have to determine what we can pay for and we must improve our archaic tax system. The real estate tax is hitting the limit." A report to the 1959 governors' conference stated: "Many people have said the local property owners have about reached the saturation point in the amount of property taxes they can absorb."

Although there have been many inquiries into the possibility of improving the tax system, it has usually been tacitly agreed that no really major changes in present systems should be considered, that political considerations would make them impossible. For example, in Britain a royal commission on this subject was confined by its terms of reference to a re-examination of present methods—suggestions for major changes were barred. It seems clear, however, that tinkering with present methods will be insufficient in the long run; it will be necessary to look for a system that will allow governments to obtain the needed funds with the least unfavorable effects and the maximum of social justice.

The problems of devising an adequate tax system are threefold. First, we must decide on the appropriate principles for taxation: in particular we must settle the proportion of taxes that should be paid by rich and poor. Secondly, we have the problem of securing adoption of any changes that prove necessary. Finally, we must try to make sure that the change from one system to another does not cause excessive hardship for any person or section of the population.

Perhaps the basic belief in the field of taxation is a preference for direct taxation as opposed to indirect. This can be traced—once more—to neoclassical economics. It was shown that direct taxes would not distort the economic pattern, while indirect taxes would. But in present conditions the price system is already distorted by "power" and by government spending, for taxes at present levels will in themselves inevitably distort the rewards and costs that would apply in a free-market situation. We should, therefore, plan tax systems so that the distortion has the minimum unfavorable and the maximum favorable results.

The economies of the rich countries now operate in such a way that growth is the almost inevitable result of the continuance of the present pattern—assuming that slumps are not allowed to develop. Firms set their prices at a level that will pay for much of the future expansion of the firm. The purchaser of goods normally *not only* pays for the labor and capital costs incorporated in the product; he *also* contributes money for the growth of the firm, enabling the directors of the company to purchase new buildings, new machinery, and to carry out research and development.

Neoclassical economics assumed that people paid the "just" price for goods and the "right" price for the labor, capital, and land incorporated in the product. It was argued that only when there was disequilibrium in the market could a profit be gained, and the possibility of a disequilibrium state was assumed to be impermanent. In actual fact companies today are often able to continue to price their goods at a level that will produce sufficient profit to pay for much or all of future needed expansion. As the consumer must pay the price set by the company if he wants to buy, industry has developed *taxing* power over the consumer, a power subject to no outside control. This method of taxation has enormous scope. Daniel Bell stated in an already-quoted article in *Commentary* that over 85 per cent of General Motors' increase in net worth during the period 1947–57 came from profits plowed back into the company rather than from sales of stock.

The failure to understand the realities behind this pattern of pricing and the continuation of analysis along the old lines has made much examination of pricing policies almost entirely irrelevant. The Senate committee hearings on the pricing patterns of the drug industry in the United States failed to develop a meaningful result because no standards could be drawn up that would specify the proper level of profits. It was true, as the committee members argued, that the prices charged for many types of drugs allowed a very large margin for profit. It was equally true, as many of the witnesses from the industry argued, that the price of drugs had to provide an adequate return that would allow the drug companies to continue to exist and support research and development work. The discussion failed to be meaningful because economics has developed no guidelines that would describe the level of profit necessary in various industries when product lives are short and, above all, uncertain.

The contrast between the methods used to raise money for industry and those used to raise money for government is striking. While much of the money used in the expansion of industry is obtained when the goods are sold—i.e., as part of the process of the economy—money for government use is usually obtained from outside the process of the economy. Industry's taxes are hidden; government taxes are open and are often almost aggressively displayed. Even in cases where people's contributions to the government could be disguised, as would be true when sales taxes are levied, these taxes are usually listed separately on the bill.

Few European powers make such a fetish of ensuring that any contribution to government will be obvious, but even in these countries the contrast between the almost complete invisibility of contributions to the expansion of industry and the visibility of contributions to governments results in a substantial bias in the use of funds. Industry has far less difficulty in obtaining the money it requires than governments who have to fight hard to obtain any increases in revenue. Galbraith has suggested that this can be overcome only by the extended use of sales taxes.

"The relation of the sales tax to the problem of social balance is admirably direct. The community is affluent in privately produced goods. It is poor in public services. The obvious solution is to tax the former to provide the latter—by making private goods more expensive, public goods are made more abundant. . . . This forthright solution has the further advantage that sales taxation can be employed with fair efficiency by states and even by cities."

We will return to the political implications of industrial "taxing" power in Chapter 9. At this point we need only consider how we can nullify the advantage industry gains from its hidden tax system. We cannot remove the right of industry to set its own prices, and therefore to decide on its level of taxation, without changing our whole industrial system. Thus this advantage of industry can be neutralized only by allowing government to hide its taxes too. A large number of people oppose hidden government levies in the belief that any extension of government services is bad and that therefore any change that makes the development of government services easier must also be bad. Government activity, however, is essential to welfare and survival. Insistence on a higher level of visibility for government taxation, as compared to industrial taxation, biases the use of resources against the government and in favor of private industry.

The remainder of this chapter is therefore devoted to sketching steps that could be taken to rationalize the tax system. It should be made clear that alterations would have to be made in an evolutionary—rather than a revolutionary—way: people have adjusted their lives to one system of taxation and any change will necessarily lead to hardship. Thus steps must be taken to avoid rapid increases in the tax burden of any families or groups, however justifiable this might at present appear.

Despite continued insistence on the merits of direct taxation by most economists, more attention is now being paid to the benefits to be derived from sales taxes. Galbraith has suggested the introduction of generalized sales, or turnover, taxes, which he correctly claims satisfy many of the conditions for an ideal tax: they are relatively easy to levy, they rise with the national income, they are subject to fairly easy adjustment when necessary. However, sales taxes usually have one major disadvantage: they impinge most heavily on the poorest members of the community. Nevertheless, this objection is not conclusive evidence that sales taxes will be unsuitable. We will have to deal with the problem of poverty whether we use sales taxes or not. Almost all observers agree that much of the remaining poverty is social and not economic in origin.

Much unemployment and underemployment are concentrated in those communities where technological progress has either led to the collapse or displacement of the industries on which the area relied or has drastically reduced the employment available in them. Such situations are found, for example, in the old New England mill towns and the coal-producing areas. The resulting social distress can often be cured only by reviving the community through subsidies. The lack of educational opportunities in some parts of the country also severely biases the prospects for those people affected. The chances of success for those without a good education are diminishing steadily. Only a reasonable standard of education for all can give everybody an equal chance in the future.

Indeed we must realize that even the present "progressive" tax system has not prevented the poorest members of society from paying a larger percentage of their income in tax than those with larger incomes. A study made in 1948 showed that, despite the progressivity of the income tax, the proportion of total revenue paid in taxes rose significantly only for incomes of $7500 and over, while those with less than $1000 paid a larger percentage in tax than those with incomes ranging from $1000 to $7500. Purposeful government action to avoid inequality of incomes is already necessary; welfare acts and minimum-wage laws are required to deal with social maladjustment. The level of benefits will have to be adjusted to take account of the sales tax, but the need for social aid will not be *caused* by the sales tax: it already exists.

Insistence on "progress" and "growth" in the Western countries has biased the collection of taxes in a particular direction. We tax existing real estate, but we do not usually tax the construction of new buildings. Taxes on existing real estate are clearly appropriate for recurring expenditures, such as the operation of schools and the police force, the repaving of roads, which must be met every year. However, in addition to annual costs of this type, the construction of new houses or factories requires capital expenditures by the local government for the construction of additional schools, additional sewage works, additional roads. It would therefore seem logical that those who carry out private construction should pay a lump sum to finance the capital costs their activities cause to the community. In this way the public expenditures *directly* attributable to private construction would be chargeable to those causing them. The need for these taxes can easily be seen when we learn that in many suburban districts the movement of new families into the area *in*creases the tax problem rather than *de*creases it. It can easily be argued that such a tax would be unscientific and unequal in effect, as it could not be "exact." But none of the present taxes is scientific in this sense, although they may seem to be, for we have come to accept the conventional wisdom that justifies their impact.

The sales tax and a levy on construction are clearly "process" taxes in the same sense as the tax system used by industry to increase the price of its goods to the consumer. There is a third type of tax that should be considered under this heading—the government tax on the incomes of corporations. It is usually argued that, just as high rates of personal income tax can severely discourage individual effort, so high rates of corporate income tax can severely discourage corporate effort. This is a false analogy. The corporation possesses an "institutionalized" set of values; perhaps the most basic of these values is the desire for the continuing growth of the corporation. The effects of a corporation income tax cannot be equated with those which result from an individual income tax: the corporation cannot afford to reduce its activities, for its profits depend on this activity. As always, the relevance of this analysis depends upon the continuance of present attitudes—a rate of taxation above a certain level could cause a basic re-examination of the role of the corporation. Nevertheless, it should be clear that the argument for a reduction in corporate tax rates is not so strongly based as is often assumed, and it seems quite possible that a moderate rate of increase might raise a considerable quantity of funds without serious side effects.

The three suggestions made above would allow an expansion in taxes. One reform that might not raise extra money is also overdue: personal income taxes in most Western countries are often too high. At the present time the highest rates may reach between 80 to 90 per cent of income. Economists now generally agree that such extreme rates are both unjust and unwise. They are unjust because two individuals with exactly the same incomes will pay very different amounts in tax—depending on their ability to benefit from expense accounts and other loopholes in the tax laws. One of the ironies of the present situation is that the richer the individual the greater his ability to reduce his effective rate of taxation by employing people to arrange his sources of income in a way that will minimize his tax liabilities. Those with smaller incomes are unable to use such techniques. There is therefore relatively general agreement that a top rate of about 50 per cent would be a sensible limit at the present time.

It is hardly likely that taxation will ever be popular however it is carried out. But some methods will be more popular and fairer than others. Any taxation reform could be carried out only after the most careful and lengthy examination. The object of this chapter is quite obviously not to provide this full examination but merely to suggest that such an examination is necessary and could be fruitful. We will see in the next chapter that there may be a need for even more drastic changes in the long run.

# 7.

## The Uses of Abundance

SOME READERS WILL certainly have challenged the assumption of the need for additional government expenditure, which lay behind the previous two chapters: they might well have made their point in the following way. "The private enterprise system has been incredibly successful in raising the standard of living of all the countries in the Western world: why alter it now?" The need for change stems from this very success. The efficiency of the private enterprise system in meeting private wants has increased the relative urgency of other needs that countries could not afford to meet in the past but that now must be satisfied. The rich countries of the world have set up an economic system that will provide an ever-increasing quantity of resources as long as social attitudes remain unchanged. The traditional delimitation of the role of the corporation and the government has caused this outpouring of goods to increase the standard of living of the individual more than it has improved the services available to the community as a whole. We discuss in this chapter the possibility of redrawing the boundaries separating the private individual, the firm, and the community along lines more appropriate to the age in which we live.

The necessity for a change stems partly from the increased ability to satisfy private wants and partly from changes in conditions of life. As a result of the first alteration, situations that in the past had to be accepted must now be regarded as intolerable. As long as there was an acute shortage of the necessities of life, government could not undertake to relieve all undeserved hardship—individual or communal. It was impossible to provide the unemployed with a decent standard of living when they were unable to find jobs through no fault of their own. Adequate medical care could not be guaranteed for all, without reference to income, because there were insufficient hospitals, doctors, and drugs. But in an economy of abundance such situations can, and certainly should, be corrected. The excuse that we cannot afford such innovations is no longer valid. The fear that we may decrease the rate of growth is no longer relevant, for we have seen that income will continue to rise.

While effective government action has been made possible by the increasing wealth of the country, the need for action has also been intensified by the changing pattern of living—in particular the shift from rural to urban areas. The rural areas need few "community" services, for most problems can be effectively solved by the family: where co-operation is needed, *voluntary* institutions often exist. In the towns, however, many of the basic needs can be satisfied only by planned community action: past failure to provide suitable institutions in these fields has a far more serious effect on welfare than any existing lack of private goods. It can hardly be doubted that the inauguration of an efficient transit system, a satisfactory police force, an adequate slum-clearance program, a good education system, or even of a beautification program for cities would add more to the satisfaction of most citizens than the private purchases they could make with the same funds.

Formal economic theory would, of course, claim that this was not true. It would be argued that, if consumers really wanted communal services more than private goods, they would get together to demand them. There is, however, an inherent bias in the economic system because of its split between the public and private sectors. This gives a major advantage to the private firm, when it seeks to expand, as compared to the government. We will see in Chapter 9 that existing political systems also limit the ability of the citizen to make clear his desire for increased community services.

The development of slums and similar phenomena stems in part from the failure to develop the types of grouping that would allow neighbors to co-operate in achieving local ends. In the rural areas both informal groups and the local government are deeply concerned with the *immediate* needs of their constituents. In the cities, government is very often the "enemy"; it is certainly hardly ever concerned with really "local" issues except on an administrative level. There is little opportunity for the individual who is deeply concerned with the problems of his district to express his ideas and put them into action. There is a need for political and/or social organizations on a very small scale, groups that will allow the inhabitants of a small area to get together to discuss common problems, so that real co-operation for common ends becomes possible. Many would certainly doubt whether such local government would work, but areas have been able to improve the conditions of their neighborhoods, and at least one block in New York has been able to reverse the drift toward slum conditions by the formation of such a council.

It is true that such steps could allow too much control over the pattern of living. It would be foolish to deny this possibility, but it is equally clear that the vital need is to find a way to reintegrate the inhabitants of an area into a "community." We are becoming familiar with the feeling of helplessness that overcomes the individual who finds his neighborhood declining but has nowhere else to go. This could be overcome in many cases by an institutional pattern that would allow people to control their own destiny. It is now only too well known that, as long as the abolition of slums is attempted by a central agency, the problem can hardly ever be solved, for the creation of new slums takes place more rapidly than the elimination of the old ones. It would surely be worth trying a program that would inhibit the formation of slums rather than replace them after they had developed.

Slums develop when people are not interested in preserving their district from decay. For this reason the destruction of old slum housing and the movement into new buildings have often only resulted in new slum housing. It seems probable that a sense of pride is necessary to keep neighborhoods attractive. Relocation can break the old sense of community that prevented a neighborhood, however poor, from degenerating rapidly while still not creating a sense of having a stake in the new area. ACTION (the American Council To Improve Our Neighborhoods) has therefore worked to reverse the process of slum formation by a national program urging owners to work within their own communities to maintain them.

Voluntary communal action, while helpful, and indeed

vital, to success in many areas, cannot be sufficient. The government will have to make more funds available through taxation. The pressure on the federal government to step up its arms expenditures has lessened its willingness and ability to support welfare programs. As a result state and local authorities have had to take on many new burdens and their sources of funds have been unbearably strained. While private philanthropy and charity remain important forces in this area, their impotence to provide an adequate and balanced program is being increasingly demonstrated. In dollars of constant value, expenditures per head in these fields have only risen some 50 per cent since 1909, and a consistently smaller proportion of disposable income has been given for these purposes in post-World War II years than in prewar years. The limitations on the scope of private charity are enhanced by the fact that individuals are no longer able to gain vast fortunes in relation to total national wealth, as was possible at the end of the nineteenth century and the beginning of the twentieth.

While the importance of private charity has been declining, a new source of funds has been developing. Industry in recent years has been making contributions to philanthropy and education. Industry, in defiance of economic theory, now collects much of its funds for expansion from the consumer and uses the funds thus collected for contributions to social goals that the directors of companies think important. The "tax" system of the private company is not solely used for its own economic goals—it also influences the *social* development of the country. Over 50 per cent of the funds raised by appeals in Toronto often come from business firms. The corporation is no longer *solely* a profit-making institution. It has become a body reflecting the social ideas and ideals of the community within which it is situated.

The proper relation between the corporation and the government must be redefined. It is no longer sufficient to define the corporation as subservient to the government, for in many situations they are clearly co-operating forces. The problem of the relationship between them is compounded by a further development that has been attracting considerable attention in recent years—the fact that control of the firm has shifted from the stockholder to the director of the company itself and is now shifting again—this time into the hands of the directors of pension funds, mutual funds, and trust funds. In America the pension funds alone are growing at a rate of four billion dollars a year: their purchases of stocks are equivalent to about 30 per cent of the total annual net additions to stocks outstanding. In England a government report has stated that insurance and pension funds constitute by far the largest single source of new capital, the net rate of accumulation of the two groups of institutions being over one and a half billion dollars a year.

As long as the ownership of shares continued in the hands of private investors who could—at least in theory—vote and thus influence the policy of the corporation, it proved possible to ignore the fact that control had *really* passed into the hands of directors. With control passing once more it is clear that the problem must be reconsidered, for the director of one company will have the power to determine the actions of other firms.

This was one of the real domestic issues of the last election —even if many of its implications were ignored. How should the relationship between government and private industry be arranged? James Reston, of the New York *Times*, put the question in the following form in an article written early in 1960. "What do the sixties require: more *consolidation*—a continuation of roughly the same foreign, defense, and do-

mestic programs—or more *innovation* to meet the social, political, industrial and military revolutions of the day?

"This question divides the reflective men and women of
both parties much more than has yet appeared on the sur-
face, for it raises in an acute form that oldest of all American
political controversies: whether the power of the Federal
Government should be increased to guarantee the security of
the American people, or held to a minimum to ensure their
freedom."

Views can be found on all sides of this question; some demanding additional government action, some stating that
only the private firm can perform the task of making America
great. One of the widest statements of the latter point of view
came in a speech made by Ralph Cordiner, chairman of General Electric, when he said: "It is worthwhile, at this point, to
review the advantages of decentralized or private planning
over state planning. In a nation such as ours, where the political freedoms of the individual are protected, particularly
the right to vote the government in and out of office, planning by government is always subject to considerations not
necessarily related to solution of the problem.

"Long-range needs of the public are frequently subordinated to the individual politician's interpretations of the
party's short-range needs for more votes. Government long-
range plans are subject to change, as control shifts from one
party to another or as parties strive for political advantages. . . .

"This is democracy, and its advantages outweigh its annoyances. But it is clear that leadership in long-range planning—
especially where time periods longer than current election
cycles are involved—needs to be sought in other quarters."

The real issue goes even deeper than this, for the difference
between government and private industry is far more limited

than is generally realized. Each has power over people, a power that gravely limits freedom of action. We discuss this in Chapter 10. Each has its own taxation system. Each affects the distribution of income in the country and by its decisions determines which social causes will flourish and which will falter. We will examine in Chapter 9 the sources from which each group obtains its power—both in theory and in practice. We will find that neither reflects the "will of the people" very closely today.

In this chapter, however, we are concerned with the problem of the "right" distribution of income; we must decide how government and industry *should* affect this distribution. At the present time the incomes of labor and management, the wages of workers in services and in industry, and those of highly skilled and unskilled workers are based on custom and convention rather than on any theory about the right distribution of wealth. It is claimed that salaries and wages, interest and rents, etc., necessarily reflected the value of workers, capital, and land, but this claim is based on a neoclassical theory that no longer has relevance.

The old rules are breaking down. Our economic system has depended on the assumption of scarcity: we paid owners of capital because they were willing to lend their money rather than use it themselves; we paid workers because there was a demand for more work than could be accomplished. We can now look forward to the day—whether it be twenty, fifty, or a hundred years off—when these conditions will no longer exist. Value depends on scarcity in the Western economic system: not on the relative necessity of the products. Thus gem diamonds, which are scarce and useless—except for prestige— can command a higher value than water or bread, which are essential for the preservation of life. Indeed, we get air free because there is sufficient for all needs. In our present economic system all products tend to become more valuable as they become scarcer, and less valuable as they become abundant. In effect, therefore, we pay more when there are not enough goods to go around. If we imagine an economy of abundance in which scarcity has been largely eliminated, we would not need to pay for many types of goods, for the elimination of scarcity would make them "valueless." However, some means would still have to be found to allocate certain resources that are inherently limited—such as space in the middle of a city.

We are in grave danger of allowing our present system to force us into unsatisfactory policies as we move from an economy of scarcity to an economy of abundance. Prices of goods normally tend downward when they become more abundant; we have seen how the recent technological revolution has led to a fall in the price of farm products. However, it is generally agreed that we cannot—within the present social system—allow this tendency to operate unchecked, for the result of a decline in the prices of the goods sold by a firm or an individual is a decline in income. It is this relationship between price and income that makes America's agricultural surpluses a major problem instead of allowing us to treat them as the first favorable signs of abundance.

At the present time the incomes of producers of goods depend entirely on the prices they obtain for their goods. Thus every producer must strive to keep his prices as high as possible in order to raise his income. As long as this system continues, it is impossible to allow prices to fall very heavily in one particular sector, as they naturally would with the possibility of increasing abundance, for the result of this fall in price would mean a decline in the incomes of those who produced them.

While the agricultural producers have been suffering from

the decreases in prices due to the rapid increase in production of their goods, the manufacturing and mining sectors have worked out systems that enable them to limit the production of goods and thus keep prices up even though the capacity may be available to allow increased production. The manufacturer produces as much as people will buy at the price he has determined; he does not produce all the goods he can and then allow prices to be set by the market. We can hardly be content with this situation, which allows some factories, mills, and oil wells to produce at 50 per cent of capacity rather than to produce all the output that could be used by the society. We must find a new dynamic solution— one that will take account of the fact that there will be a steadily increasing quantity of goods available in coming years. The system must therefore not only provide for justice at a point in time but must also allow for the distribution of increasing amounts of goods in the future.

The basic economic fact of coming years is that the available supply of goods will *inevitably* rise. This potential increase can be taken up in two ways. First, attempts can be made to encourage the adoption of a steadily higher standard of living; the larger quantity of available goods could be absorbed by steadily rising purchases. There is, however, growing concern about the effects of making the major goal of any society that of the most rapid possible expansion in material wealth; there is increasing doubt whether this process will augment happiness, and also fear that this goal may disrupt society. We return to this subject in Chapter 10.

It remains true that huge sums are needed for education, for rebuilding slums and indeed whole cities, for health, and for a multitude of other ends. But the potential need must be placed in perspective. The average annual increase in the national income in America could be of the order of $25 billion in 1961, $40 billion in 1970, and $70 billion in 1980. The increase in the national income in the 1960's alone will be larger than the total national income at the end of World War II. Our increasing production will allow us to meet our needs without *mobilizing* our societies to this end.

The admitted need for money in the poor countries cannot alter this general picture, for there are very real limits to the amount of funds these countries can absorb. These limitations stem primarily from the same essential problem that must determine action in the rich countries—the need to preserve the structure of society rather than destroy it. Even if the rich countries were to adopt an *unlimited* commitment to help the poor countries to the fullest possible extent, the amount that could be absorbed by the poor countries would not rise above 2 per cent of the national incomes of the rich countries within the foreseeable future.

A second method of dealing with the increased potential supply would be to decrease the number of hours of work devoted to the production of goods and increase the number of hours devoted to "leisure." Such a solution has many advantages, and it seems clear that the long-run movement in hours of work should be downward. But it may be doubted that this change should be brought about too rapidly, for we have still failed to develop meaningful leisure. As a result, the problem of boredom in the United States and to a lesser extent in other parts of the industrial world is already extremely serious. It still remains true that the happy man is very often the one who has insufficient time to worry about whether he is happy or not. We have misconstrued the problem: leisure is not an amount of time spent *not* working, but a state of mind. In a recent article in *Harper's Magazine*, Charlton Ogburn, Jr., suggested that the American did not understand leisure. "Much is being made over the growing amount of leisure in American life. In fact, however, leisure is alien to us. The time we save with the latest in laborsaving machinery we characteristically spend in filling our lives with more noise and movement. According to the pollsters, the number of Americans who claim to be reading a book is only half the number who own an automobile. Leisure, contrary to what we may believe, is not what is left over after a forty-hour week; it is a spirit, an outlook on life. Charles Morgan defined it when he observed, 'The party had that quality of ease and leisure which is peculiarly Italian, none of the guests having an axe to grind, an appointment to keep, or any desire to excel.' It wasn't an American party."

A very large number of people would claim that the highest possible rate of growth was needed in order to "beat the Russians." This process may be defined to include the need for more scientific knowledge, more education, a faster rate of space exploration, more armaments. Some of these goals are, of course, valuable in themselves, but we are concerned here with the argument that they should be pushed because of their importance in "winning" the cold war. Few, if any, of those who have examined the problems of international relations believe that the present system of bipolar forces can continue for an unlimited time into the future. All agree that a system of world organization based on a struggle between two great powers or power blocs is necessarily unstable. While few would argue that this means that we should cease to compete at the present time, it does mean that we cannot postulate the continuing need for economic growth on this factor over a long period.

We must re-examine the benefits of economic growth, a subject we will discuss from a philosophical viewpoint in Chapter 10. At this point we are concerned with the economic justification of progress and in particular with the basic economic assumption that if a step proves to be profitable from the point of view of a person or a firm it will necessarily be good for the community. We have seen that the corporation must develop new materials and new products if it is to prosper. Is it necessarily true that a change that is found desirable by a firm will be an improvement for an area, country, or the world as a whole?

We can examine first the development of a new type of product that makes other brands obsolete. Let us take, for example, the introduction of a new pen. The company that developed the new pen will try to introduce it onto the market if it is convinced that their new product will sell and make a profit for the company. Let us assume that the company is successful. Their pen takes over the market of another manufacturer, whose sales drop. In the end he is forced out of business, his workers must look for new jobs, and his machinery becomes almost worthless. Retailers will try to sell cheaply their stocks of the now discontinued line and will lose money. The manufacturer of the new pen is unconcerned by all these developments, for they do not affect his profit—only *his* success is important. He can ignore the loss suffered elsewhere. But if we consider the welfare of society as a whole, the gain from the introduction of the new pen will not always cover the loss consequent upon its introduction. It should be noted that the assumptions made here are basic to the analysis. There will be many cases when the introduction of new goods is equally or even more profitable for society than for the manufacturer himself. We are only concerned to demonstrate that the profit gained by the manufacturer *can* be greater than the advantage obtained by society.

That this analysis is relevant can be seen by examining the policy of the telephone companies, which must consider the effect of new equipment on their total investment throughout the country. The companies make few changes, adopting new equipment only after it has been thoroughly tested and proved and, if possible, they delay the introduction until the old equipment it will replace has reached the end of its useful life. The company cannot ignore any of the costs of introducing equipment, for, being a largely self-contained system, it must bear all of them itself.

The almost continuous building program in many parts of the rich countries also causes problems of measurement. Buildings are torn down to make room for new ones, although the old ones are still perfectly adequate. There is, of course, a potential profit in the transaction, for unless this were true the change would not be made. However, the profit is often gained at the cost of forcing the payment of moving expenses onto the tenants and by ignoring the monetary value of the inconvenience and cleaning expenses caused by the demolition and subsequent rebuilding. If all additional costs were considered, it is probable that in many cases it would prove more profitable for society to allow the old building to remain standing for a further period of years.

This type of problem exists on an international scale, as can be seen if we examine the ways in which present research has affected and is likely to continue to change the prospects of the poor countries. We have seen that all a company needs in order to adopt a change is the prospect of profit for itself; it is not interested in the losses it may cause for others. This distribution between the profit of one firm and the losses caused in other economies can be particularly serious when methods of making synthetics are discovered that will replace production in the poor countries.

The possible development of synthetic coffee poses a serious threat in this area. Natural coffee has been subject to periodic

gluts throughout its history—gluts that became extremely serious during the 1930's. Evidence is now building up that a
similar glut is likely to occur during the 1960's. Conditions
are steadily worsening as countries encourage production and
as some of the international organizations make loans to increase coffee production in certain areas. Brazil's surplus
alone would be sufficient to provide normal imports for the
whole world for a year. Meanwhile, a report to the Senate by
the Stanford Research Institute stated, "A number of labora-
tories in this country and abroad are presently seeking to
identify the flavor compounds present in coffee. Published research results indicate that over 30 volatile compounds have
been identified, and that a mixture of the components already identified gave an aroma similar to the original natural
essence. The analysis, it was reported, was still not complete,
but would undoubtedly be completed in coming years, if not
in coming months."

It is certain that any reasonable accounting system that
took into consideration the social dislocation and disruption
in the poor countries that would be caused by the introduction of synthetic coffee in the rich would lead to the conclusion that this would not be favorable. However, our present
economic system has no provision for any method that would
make such a step possible—people and firms can cause major
damage to the economy in order to secure a limited profit for
themselves. We need to develop techniques that will make it
possible to bring the costs to the private person and firm into
closer accord with the costs to society.

One of the first steps necessary to cause this result will be
to downgrade the importance given to national income calculations. Our faith in present statistics is such that we consider an increase in national income as necessarily good with-

out any further examination. This is unrealistic, for our methods of calculation are most peculiar. We can see just how odd they are by examining the effect of the rebuilding program discussed above. We saw that this rebuilding would cause costs to the tenants and to those in neighboring buildings. However, payments for moving from one building to another and payment for additional cleaning, repainting, etc., made necessary by the demolition appear by some alchemy as an *addition* to and not a *subtraction* from the national income. Any *expenditure* increases the national income. A rise in salaries of civil servants without any change in the work they do will also raise the national income. We need new methods of calculation that will reflect more accurately the real changes in wealth.

It may be helpful to summarize these chapters that have dealt with the economic condition of the rich countries. The rich countries have produced a social and economic order in which an ever-increasing quantity of material goods will be produced. This growth in production is now largely independent of the "individual" reactions of people; the institutionalized values of the firm and the society compel certain actions. But efficiency and production per man hour can be dramatically improved in only certain types of jobs; in others there can be little or no change. For example, the "efficiency" of judges and teachers has not changed greatly since the beginning of the century.

Society as a whole has decided that the benefits of the increase in the available standard of living should not be confined to those occupations in which productivity is increasing most rapidly, but should be spread among all occupations; thus there is generalized support for the idea that no group should be left behind in the progress toward higher standards. The standard of living available to clerks and bus drivers, lawyers and teachers has been increased by general consent.

Our acceptance of this increase in standards for all rests, however, on an incomplete understanding of what is happening. We still ask the question "What are these services worth?" rather than "What should society pay for these services?" The resolution of these two questions is very different. The productivity of certain types of workers has not increased: their services are therefore not objectively worth more than before. The basic change is that the society can now afford to pay more. Under these circumstances decisions about the exact amount that should be paid for various types of services cannot be left to market forces, but depend on abstract ideas about the right distribution of income.

What principles should inspire decisions on these subjects? What guarantees should be given to all the citizens of a rich country so that none should suffer acute penury through the working of a system they are no longer able to control? Can the rich countries afford today the shame of city slums and depressed industrial areas? Can we allow lives to be ruined because of the financial hardship from an illness the sufferer could not have prevented?

The doctrine of non-interference by government is sometimes claimed as necessary for the continuation of the free society. Indeed it would often appear as though certain propagandists suggest that *any* system that would provide adequate free health care would inevitably lead to dissolution of the American dream. Despite the peripheral complaints that have surrounded the National Health Service in Britain it is true to say that only a minute fraction of the people would be willing to return to a situation in which the standard of medical care depended on one's income. The system is not perfect. Many changes could be made that would improve it. Nevertheless, it is overwhelmingly agreed that the gain in human dignity that attended the introduction of the health service more than compensated for any unfavorable side effects it produced.

How should we provide reasonable standards for all? It has been suggested that the payment of unemployment benefits should be revised so that payments should rise when the unemployed were least to blame for their idleness—during a slump. Society should recognize the fact that *some* people will inevitably be unemployed during a slump and that they must be supported by society. While each person could find a job if he made more effort or were lucky, he could do so only at the cost of depriving some other person of his work.

The West has "defined" its societies as being based on scarcity, and the economic system we have devised enhances and perpetuates this scarcity. Even our calculation of national income assumes scarcity. However, if we are moving into an economy of abundance, we must develop a pattern that will allow the emergence of abundance. Our present system forces manufacturers to limit the production of goods as soon as "market" demand is satisfied. Surplus industrial and agricultural capacity develops, but it cannot be used.

The problems of the present system can be best illustrated by the farm crisis: a crisis of overproduction. In the present topsy-turvy world the ability to produce more food than we require is not an advantage but a disaster. Why is this so? The natural result of surplus production is a decline in price: the decline in the price limits the income of those producing the goods, and thus their standard of living. The agricultural crisis stems, therefore, not from the overproduction itself but from the fact that the farmer's income falls with overproduction.

We can allow the price of goods to fall only if this change does not damage the interests of the producers too greatly. This in turn will be possible only when we revise the nature of the present tie between production and income. In the last century and a half we have tried to solve two problems with a single mechanism. We have allowed the income received from the production of goods to determine the distribution of wealth. However, this system is no longer suitable for an economy moving toward abundance. The economy of abundance will have rules different from those applying in an economy of scarcity. *The fact that a proposed solution would be impossible in an economy of scarcity does not mean that it is not appropriate for an economy of abundance.*

We can end this part of the book with a suggestion that would make possible a move into an economy of abundance. This idea has been little canvassed, but it stems from the basic ideals of the American Revolution. Jefferson believed there could be no freedom without private property, that without private property each man was the "slave" of his employer and the currently accepted views of society. This remains a basic truth, for without independent means a man can seldom afford to dissent. The society of abundance could, at last, provide independent means, which would allow each individual to obtain minimum amounts of clothing, food, and shelter. They would not keep the family in luxury but would provide the necessities of life. The unemployed would be assured of a reasonable standard of living. The student, the writer, the artist, the visionary, the dissenter could live on this income if they considered their work sufficiently important.

There can be no doubt that the first reaction to such a suggestion must necessarily be "negative," for it destroys many of the shibboleths on which we have based our lives. One complaint would state that there would inevitably be an increase in shiftlessness. Another that there would be insufficient people willing to work. A third that everybody *should* have a proper job and not be allowed to waste his time. However, in the context of a society of abundance these complaints become irrelevant.

There have been societies where "abundance" has been largely achieved in the past. As late as the end of the nineteenth century the Burmese allowed their crops to rot in the fields rather than harvest and market them. Such a society was possible only with the acceptance of limited desires. We too can have a society of abundance in the rich countries before the end of the twentieth century. But abundance is not a specific quantity of goods; it is a state of mind, a set of attitudes. Man could *never* produce *all* he could use; abundance depends on the *acceptance* of a reasonable standard of living. The next three chapters trace the changes necessary for such a situation to be possible, and suggest that our acceptance of a limited rate of growth is necessary if we are to preserve responsible freedom—the prime value of the West.

**PART II**

*The Social Challenge*

# 8.

## Education for a Changing World

WHAT IS EDUCATION? Sometimes one is tempted to believe that there are almost as many definitions of the purposes of education as there are educators. Our views about its aims have certainly not kept pace with the changes in conditions that have been discussed in previous chapters. In order to understand what education can and should do in a society of abundance, we must examine how children grow up to be members of a society and the changes that must be made if we are to bring up the present generation not only to survive in new conditions but to understand and control them.

Each society has a particular set of values—some inherited from the past, some developed in response to changing conditions. The values of each society are different, although the gap between the philosophies of societies may be relatively limited. For example, all the Western societies share a belief in the value of work and a higher standard of living. In other cases the values of two groups may be so different that a person brought up in one group will hardly be able to understand those of the other.

Education in its broadest sense is the process of enabling a person to live in his own society. The patterns of behavior, the ideas and ideals of a person, will depend on the values of the society in which he grew up. A person brought up by Chinese would behave like the Chinese, a German brought up in America away from the influence of his own culture would behave like an American. In actual fact, of course, many people develop under the influence of several different sets of values: an American child living in India would grow up under the influence of his parents *and* of the traditional Indian pattern. The Japanese whose parents emigrated to America often suffers from the considerable conflict between the patterned family life of the Japanese and the less circumscribed culture in America.

The values held by children, therefore, depend largely on the society in which they grow up. People in different parts of the world will accept different ways of behavior. An analogy may make this point clearer. The essential assumption of "liberal" doctrines is that one can see the world without any form of bias, that there is an objective pattern. Social scientists generally agree that this is not so—they believe that the culture suggests patterns of thought to the individual that enable him to make sense of his world. It is as though each society had different sets of spectacle lenses; each arranging the world into a particular pattern. The process of education consists in large part in the fitting of these lenses. Unfortunately our educational systems can fail; they may give the individual no glasses whatsoever, in which case the world appears an undecipherable blur, or they may leave him with bi- or trifocals so that he sees different parts of life with different lenses, with blurring where they overlap. Only in a very few cases does education succeed at the present time in developing a set of lenses that permits the individual to perceive the cultures of the world in focus.

Which of these lenses is "best"? Anthropologists and sociologists generally agree that there is no objective way of determining whether one form of social organization is intrinsically "better" than others. They agree that it may well be possible to show that one form of social, economic, and political organization is most efficient as a means of achieving certain goals. For example, an increasing number of people would argue that only a social pattern similar to that in the developing countries will make it possible to achieve a really rapid rate of growth. But this does not prove that the goal of a continually higher standard of living is a suitable one for the greatest satisfaction of mankind.

Children are brought up to accept the goals that the society has developed for itself in the past. There is therefore an element of circularity in any attempt to develop goals. If we ask a group of Americans, brought up with American values, to determine what the "good life" may be, their conclusions will necessarily be strongly affected by the ideas already accepted in their society. Economic growth and larger "freedom" through this economic growth will certainly be a major component of the policies they suggest. On the other hand, many of those in the Far East and in other poor countries still will not admit that the production of an abundance of material goods should be an end in itself. They will agree on the necessity and importance of economic growth—given the present conditions—but they will deny that it will lead to satisfaction for mankind. Unfortunately, many groups are unwilling to admit that the views of others may be as good as their own, they insist that foreign countries are ill-informed, and will often go further and accuse others of falsifying their real thoughts for propaganda purposes. The thought patterns of different societies can be so different that one society finds it difficult to believe that another can genuinely believe in goals so different from its own.

This particular problem has existed from the time different groups came into contact, but a new development has occurred in recent years to complicate the whole subject. We can no longer treat the "values" and "goals" of each society as fixed points. In earlier centuries we could determine our policies in the light of past goals that had been hallowed by time. This is no longer possible because of the rate of technical and economic change. The great debate on national purpose that is being carried on in many countries stems from our realization that the values and goals we have used to organize our lives in the past are no longer really relevant to our problems and that we must find new ideals if we wish to survive. Because this process of changing our goals has never been necessary in the past, we have not yet discovered a way of carrying on a meaningful debate on this subject. Discussion of these problems—when it does take place—is still often dismissed as unnecessary or condemned as a waste of time that could be better used for "practical" purposes. However, purposes are practical only in so far as they contribute to the goals of society: until we know our goals any decisions may equally well move us away from the ends we should seek rather than toward them.

We must develop new techniques of teaching that will allow for alterations in facts and enable us to incorporate developments in theoretical formulations into new thought patterns and values. One scientific example will show the need for change in this area. Those who received their schooling before the end of World War II normally consider matter as being made up of unsplittable atoms. They are perfectly aware—intellectually—that the atom has been split, but this does not form part of their basic pattern of thought: it has to be *superimposed* on their structure of knowledge rather than *integrated* within it. Those who have been educated in the years *since* the war live in a different world, a world that comprehends the principle and the consequences of splitting the atom: the generation now in college is aware of the impossibility of "victory" after war. Given the certainty of increasing change in theories, we must find new methods of teaching so that the basic body of ideas by which we live can be shifted around to allow us to incorporate new facts into our thought patterns rather than to superimpose them.

The problem of the right pattern of education is far more complex than we wish to admit. Education shapes the ideas and ideals of each child. It does so in part by causing the adoption of certain attitudes: loyalty to family, loyalty to country, the importance of work. In part, it does so by the very choice of the facts taught to the child. Education cannot teach all the facts; it must classify them in such a way that they seem relevant. This is done in the physical sciences by a process of simplification. Thus, there is a law of gravity, which states that all objects will fall at the same rate—but the law applies only in a perfect vacuum. If objects fall in the atmosphere—as they usually do—the rate of fall will depend upon the resistance they offer to the air, on wind velocity, and many other factors.

The social scientist carries out a similar process when he tries to formulate laws expressing the way in which society operates, but the process is infinitely more complex. Different authorities have found it possible to construct and support theories that are flatly contradictory with each other. Even if the social scientist does succeed in developing a valid theory, he faces an additional problem seldom met by the physical scientist. For, while the conditions treated by the physical scientist seldom change, those of the social scientist are in constant flux, and a theory valid at one time will probably not apply in a later period or in different countries. Martin Mayer, in a comment on advertising, put it this way: "In all the behavioral sciences, a valid insight is good only for the moment of perception, and for an uncertain but probably short time afterwards."

Educational patterns must be altered to keep up with the increasing pace of change. While we have taught accepted theories as unchanging truth in the past, the present scientific and educational revolution on which we have now entered would make the continuation of this course disastrous. Although we can, of course, teach only in terms of present knowledge and present conditions, we must do so with full recognition of the fact that many of these theories and ideas will be superseded in the lifetime of the children who are being taught. It is no longer sufficient to tell a person *what* he should think—what theories have already been developed —he must be taught *how* to think so that he can make sense of an altering world and plan a sensible course of action whatever the conditions. This will require a revolution in education, but this drastic change must take place. We have to teach the student how people arrived at their ideas and how changes in conditions may have affected their relevance. We must teach students how to develop their own philosophy so that they will not always require support from an authority but will be willing to work out their *own* conclusions.

It is hardly necessary to state that this definition of the problem of education is a far cry from the preoccupations of many educational specialists at the present time who often seem to be chiefly concerned with the division between academic and non-academic subjects. The intellectuals distrust the schools that have given a prominent place to "training for leisure," and demand that all the available time should be set aside for the "pursuit of excellence." The distinction is invalid, for education is concerned with the whole of each person's life. The school child of today will live into an era when he will work only twenty hours a week. One of our most urgent tasks is to make this leisure time meaningful rather than boring. Only a small proportion can devote all their lives to intellectual pursuits and gain their pleasure in this way; there are many more who must be taught to enjoy other worth-while forms of leisure activities.

If education is necessary to enable man to make sense of his life, how can this education be financed? Thirteen experts who studied the probable evolution of higher education in the 1960's and reported their findings in *Financing Higher Education 1950–1970* showed that college enrollment might almost double between 1958 and 1970, while costs might rise about 150 per cent during the same period of years. Divergencies of opinion developed when the educators discussed means of financing this immense increase in costs. Some argued that much of the rise should be met by an increase in students' fees, but others doubted the practicability of this solution, arguing that the strain on family finances was already severe in many cases and would become intolerable if an increase of this magnitude were accepted.

It seems probable that this problem of adequate financing can be solved only by a thorough revision of present ideas. We must return and re-examine the principles that underlie the financing of education. It came to be accepted in the nineteenth and twentieth centuries that each child had a *right* to an education. Given the amount of resources that could be devoted to education, this right was considered terminated, by most countries, around the age of fourteen to sixteen: those children who wanted further education had to be able to pay for it themselves or had to be able to gain a fellowship or scholarship on the basis of their outstanding ability. Today, however, the rich countries can afford a longer period of education for their children: it is therefore necessary that the nation's obligation be extended to cover a further period of years. This change would not be "socialistic," but a necessary guarantee of the presently proclaimed "equality of opportunity."

In the context of the far-reaching change in the structure of the economy, suggested in the last chapter, much of the problem would be solved. We saw that one possible method of distributing income in a society of abundance would be to guarantee each individual a basic income so that he could live regardless of whether he had or even wanted a job. Within such a framework it would be possible to have the fees of all students paid by the community. Once more, this question is basically one of how a country wishes to distribute its resources. The rich countries, and particularly America, are now rich enough to arrange their distribution of wealth in many different ways. If America desires that seven million people should benefit from higher education in the year 1970, the resources can be made available. But the present methods of providing funds will not be adequate.

The problem of increased enrollment and rising costs is still further complicated by the fact that adult education will necessarily be more important in the years ahead. At the present time the full process of education consists of about ten to thirteen years of schooling, for many some three to four years of undergraduate training, and for a very few three to five years of graduate training. But after the student leaves his school or university, it is generally considered that his "education" is complete and that he can be left to gather information on later changes in conditions by himself. The ever more rapid rate of growth in knowledge means that this assumption is no longer relevant. Lewis Mumford put the problem in the following terms in the book *Brainpower Quest:* "The man who has been educated in 1956 and hasn't gone on with his self-education, beyond his immediate day-to-day activities, will be uneducated in 1976. We have to think of revising the education curriculum, along with our whole scheme of work, to plan for a life-time education for all of us who are capable of taking advantage of it. The professions may even have to organize sabbatical years for study to accomplish their larger purpose of maintaining a high level of technical efficiency without debasing, through inanition and neglect, the human values we must nourish and cherish."

This need for continued education is one of the most crucial problems of today. We must accept the fact that increasing wealth and knowledge will make changes in values necessary. However, we still do not know how we can change values to keep up with changes in conditions. Our techniques are elementary even in the so-called "logical" West, where people are sometimes open to argument; we have practically no knowledge of the methods that can be effectively used to alter values that are based not on "rationality" but on "tradition."

Max Weber provided us with verbal tools of analysis to examine the problem of changing values by his division of authority into three types: the administrative, the traditional, and the charismatic. Administrative authority is based on a set of laws: traditional authority relies on what has been done in the past. Both these systems tend to reinforce presently accepted patterns, although the administrative pattern is far more flexible and on-going than the traditional. Charismatic authority, Weber's third category, uses the personal magnetism possessed by a single leader and changes thought patterns through the devotion of his followers to him and to all he is considered to represent. Weber suggests that this charismatic quality is necessary if change is to take place, particularly in regions where behavior has previously been based on "tradition." But he points out that "charismatic" authority is often revolutionary and frequently under feeble control. He suggests that charismatic leadership is also likely to set off conflicts with other groups, conflicts that may have serious consequences in today's acutely interdependent world.

This danger is particularly severe in present conditions. The world is considered to be divided into two mutually exclusive patterns of thought: one "democratic" and one "communist." Although the true charismatic leader will not follow either pattern, there is a grave danger that both the West and the East will try to refuse such a leader the "right" to follow his own path. Thus Ghana's and Guinea's unwillingness to follow the straight U.S. policy line in the United Nations in 1960 was described by various American authorities as showing that the two countries were going communist: an interpretation that was very likely to bring about the result America was trying to avoid. This was shown by Kwame Nkrumah's reaction to these comments: he left the United Nations General Assembly seriously concerned about the naïveté of the American officials who insisted that he was swinging to the left simply because he failed to agree with the policies they proposed. We must realize that the problems of the underdeveloped countries cannot be solved by either pure Western or pure communist methods: we must allow each country to search for its own techniques and methods.

Arnold Toynbee also places the responsibility for change upon a few "superhuman" individuals. For him the bulk of the population must learn by "mimesis," i.e., by "absorbing" the changed ideas their leaders have developed. Toynbee makes his reasoning clear in the following passage: "The direct kindling of creative energy from soul to soul . . . is no doubt the ideal way. Yet to enjoin this way exclusively is a counsel of perfection. The problem of bringing the uncreative rank and file of a growing society into line with the creative pioneers, in order to save the pioneers' own advance from being brought to a halt, cannot be solved in practice, on the social scale, without also bringing into play the faculty of sheer mimesis—one of the less exalted faculties of Human Nature which has more in it of drill than of inspiration."

We now know that man forms his ideas through his cultural traditions: we have become aware at the same time that we will change man by changing these traditions. Our knowledge has made intervention inevitable. In the future we intervene just as fully by failing to make a decision—i.e., by allowing existing forces to continue unchecked—as we do by positive action. What must be the sense of our action? It is this subject we discuss in the two following chapters.

It should be clear that the tenor of this discussion suggests that the goals of education must be very broad: that education must aim to make life meaningful. In one of the most discussed books on education to be published in recent years, *The House of Intellect,* Jacques Barzun suggested that the result of education should be to produce a capacity for calculating judgment. According to Barzun, the educated man or intellectual should find the detection of error more important than common humanity—he seems to believe that intellect is not for the service of man but is to be served by man. "The threat of 'great ideas' to the peaceful conduct of ordinary life is plain: compromise, bargains, tolerance, the salutary neglect of trivial acts—all these are at once ruled out. Intellect is rigid and allows no oversight." This is the same error that has overtaken so many scientists. Just as scientific truth does not overrule the need for science to serve man, neither does intellectual truth rule out the use of compromise to serve man. In fact, as we will see in later chapters, the use of intellect will show that it is only through the development of the art of compromise that the world can hope to survive.

The intellect is only one part of man's equipment for dealing with his problems. We do not compromise or demean the intellectual faculty if we allow it to be mixed with passion or compassion. There is never one answer that is *intellectually* right, a second that is *politically* right, and a third *compassionately* right. We often do not know the right answer, and man may never know it, but this does not mean that there can be a multiplicity of right answers.

Nathan Pusey has defined the real role of the scholar; his words are highly appropriate as an end to this chapter on education: "We live in a time of such rapid change and growth in knowledge that only he who is in a fundamental sense a scholar—that is, a person who continues to learn and inquire—can hope to play the role of guide. Indeed it is not too much to believe that we may now be coming into an Age of the Scholar, for we have created for ourselves a manner of living in America in which a little learning can no longer serve our needs."

# 9.

## *Politics in a Complex Society*

I T IS NOT possible to design a pattern for society that would avoid all conflict. The interest of individuals and groups will necessarily clash at certain points. One of the major tasks of society must therefore be to devise methods that will regulate potential or actual conflicts.

There are essentially three different methods that can be used to achieve this result: *power, negotiations,* and *law. Power* may be defined as the use of pressure or force to bend one party to a quarrel to the will of another: for example, by armed invasion, by economic sanctions, by the fear of a strike or a lockout, or by the threat of dismissal. *Negotiations* can be defined as the attempt by both sides in a conflict to decide on a compromise solution that will be best for both parties without the use of force or the threat of force. *Law* may be defined as the process of judging a situation on principles to which the two parties adhere, where decisions will be made independently of the persons involved, without regard to the possible use of force, and where both parties will abide by the decision.

Power is by far the most common means used to settle disagreements in the West. For example, labor-management bargaining is based on power. Each group tries to make the eventual result of any agreement as favorable as possible to its own views; when agreement is not reached society as a whole allows each side to use economic pressure against the other. In a similar way the Western political system is based on the use of power. This reliance on power in decision-making in the West is not paralleled in all parts of the world. Some decisions made in the West by the use of power are settled by negotiations elsewhere. We must accept that our present system is not "ideal," for it is not "justice" when decisions are made on the basis of the power that the participants to a quarrel can bring to bear rather than on the inherent merits and demerits of the case. It is at least arguable that a method that would allow for compromise between opposing views would be more satisfactory.

To those brought up in the Western tradition, a change away from the use of power toward an increased use of the processes of negotiation and law may well appear impossible. But there have been many areas of the world where decisions have been based on unanimity rather than on majority rule. People have been willing to subordinate their own interests to those of the group as a whole. Unanimity under these conditions is not the result of coercion and force, as the West generally argues, but results from a willingness to compromise.

We are seldom willing to look at our methods of political

organization with an unbiased eye. We claim that the process of labor-management bargaining, our legislative methods, our judicial procedures are all the *best* that can be devised. We are unwilling to consider them as instruments that should be used to provide the best possible way of life, but that may require change following alterations in economic and social conditions. *We have elevated institutions into values.* This process of changing methods of social organization into values in their own right is not unique to our civilization: it seems to have been the ultimate cause of the breakdown of many past societies. Vested interests have demanded the continuation of methods that were of benefit to *them,* and have refused to allow the renewal of the vitality of their societies.

Major alterations in social organization have very often been achieved by violence. The most basic task of the world in the remainder of the twentieth century is to develop a new view of society both within each country and on a world-wide scale. A second problem is to express this perception in new institutions. The chief difficulty in carrying out this task is that we can no longer afford *any major violence* as we try to bring about a new transnational view.

It is sometimes suggested that the Western countries have already accomplished a great change in values since the beginning of the twentieth century, but this underestimates the nature of the task that now confronts us. Since the beginning of the twentieth century we have been tacking new pieces of social *group* philosophy onto an *individualistic* basic philosophy. The joints of this jerry-built structure are beginning to creak, for our "social" legislation is not supported by our basic philosophy. If we are to build meaningfully, we must develop a philosophy that justifies the right of all men to a decent income, to adequate medical care, and to suitable schooling. We need a new bill of rights that will enable society to benefit as much as possible from the level of income now available in the rich countries.

This change would not relieve the individual of responsibility: it would merely place his responsibility in a different area. In the past, society has claimed that its members were entitled to a living only if they carried out a task society defined as valuable and for which it was willing to pay. The creation of a society of abundance will make it possible to relax this requirement. We will be able to allow people to follow an interest they find vital, but that society would not support through the price mechanism.

Such a suggestion is almost instinctively rejected by many, and for two very different reasons. First, they suggest that any policy that would allow the individual to obtain a living without working for it would deprive the economy of the necessary labor force. However, within the foreseeable future our problem will be to find work for all those who desire it. The second objection is that people feel that such a policy would free the individual from any responsibility to society. But this reaction occurs only because we have tended to define the responsibility of the individual to society in purely economic terms. By freeing the individual from economic responsibility we would allow him to concentrate on his duties to the community—an area we now neglect.

We must reconsider our individualistic philosophy, which grew out of ultilitarian theories and which suggests that the person who follows his own selfish interests would do no wrong. Although neither the economic nor the political theorizing that led to this result was valid, acceptance of this *in*valid theorizing *was* responsible for the industrial revolution and for the level of income that has been obtained in the rich countries. However, these theories are no longer suitable in our acutely interdependent world. We can no longer simply assume that the man who follows his own desires will benefit society. We must recognize the fact that society's needs may be more important than those of a single person.

Three basic difficulties face us as we try to develop a new social philosophy. The first is one that has applied throughout the ages, the unwillingness of man to give up his own vested interests for the good of others. However, new forces will limit this problem: the longer-range selfish interests of each person now clearly *require* closer co-operation throughout the world if profits, and even survival, are to be ensured. There is growing comprehension that modern society will operate only if all its members are willing to compromise, that a strict insistence on existing rights would lead to an intolerable situation for all.

The second problem stems from the intellectual activity needed if we are to throw off the bonds of existing thought. All of us are far more in thrall to the theories existing at the time of our education than we care to admit. We have not rearticulated human knowledge in such a way as to form a new meaningful whole. Economics provides a good example of the problems involved in this area. Each of the basic theories necessary to neoclassical economics has been disproved on several occasions. But, despite the fact that the theories are not valid, the system lives on and has even succeeded in absorbing the Keynesian challenge, forming what is called a Keynesian-neoclassical-synthesis. Similarly, the development of new disciplines has undermined the theoretical foundations on which other subjects are based, but this has not been fully recognized, for no great synthesizer has been able to produce a meaningful theory for all the disciplines, or even for one set of disciplines such as the physical *or* the social sciences. Policies continue to be based on disproved theories. Fortunately this difficulty could be overcome far more rapidly than now seems possible. There are people working in all fields toward synthesis with other disciplines. Unfortunately their efforts are not normally well supported, for the effect of a new synthesis is extremely disruptive, particularly in the social sciences, where it is likely to alter views about right forms of actions. Despite ostensible freedom of research and publication, there is little real welcome for radically new ideas, for they destroy established power positions.

There is a third difficulty in the way of revising our value systems and of producing a bill of rights appropriate for the age in which we live. Many of the policies now required by the situation have been described in the past as socialist and communist and therefore arouse widespread distrust. People will not even consider these policies: they are taboo on doctrinal grounds. The continuation of such an attitude will ensure that we are unable to evolve new methods appropriate for the age in which we live. Fortunately all the evidence points to the conclusion that less attention is now being paid to "doctrinal" factors both in the political parties and among the voters themselves. There is far more willingness to consider issues on their merits. Since 1956 the number of people who consider themselves as independent of political parties has risen from 8 to 23 per cent. The percentage of independents is notably higher among the young, the college-trained, and business and professional workers.

However, it is not only the political parties that are supporters of "political" ideologies. Each group has theories of its own; perhaps the most fully developed is that of the industrial community. This group has almost complete control over those who work within it, it is able to "tax" those who use its goods, it distributes the resources it produces, on principles it develops for itself—dividing income among labor, suppliers, stockholders, and those social causes it finds worthy of support. In fact the actual "political" role of business is wider than that which has been held to be proper for *governments* under Western theory.

We can understand the proper role for industry only after we have examined the stereotype that is accepted as describing its present role, and have contrasted this with the actual situation. The corporation is legally and generally considered as composed of people who have come together for a common purpose that will allow them—hopefully—to make money. In theory the corporation is responsible to those who put up the money and is under their control—the shareholders set policy and decide on the steps to be taken. Among the large companies and also among the small- and medium-sized firms with diffused ownership this idealized pattern has no relation to reality. Directors now control the company; the board of directors appoints its own successors and forms a self-perpetuating hierarchy.

There are, of course, exceptions to this pattern, but they are of relatively little importance to the over-all picture. The board of directors may be voted out of office in at least two possible situations. It may be ousted by a group that wants to benefit by taking over the existing assets of the company. This may occur when the value of the shares of a company are considered to be below the actual worth of its assets. In this situation a group of investors or a single person may try to buy a large enough part of the shares in order to be able to install its own directors. Secondly, a shareholder's revolt may occur following mismanagement of the company, and this may force a change in directors—or the board of directors may decide to allow or force one of the directors or even the chairman or president of the company to resign in order to quiet the opposition.

But in the vast majority of cases the directors decide on

their own goals. How are they set? The directors are clearly concerned to forward the interest of the company. However, this only puts the question back one step: What are the interests of the company? We have already seen that the more enlightened companies have been increasingly conscious of their social obligations and have been advancing social goals. The corporation, like the government, now tends to reflect the general attitudes of society. Was the now famous statement by Charles Wilson, claiming that what was good for General Motors was good for the United States, really true—even if for unexpected reasons?

The actions of the firm cannot be examined at the present time primarily on the assumption that it is a social entity, for the actions of firms must be "justified" in terms of the stereotype, i.e., in terms of the ability of any action to increase profits. It is, of course, true that the element of "profitability" may be very remote, as in the case of many contributions to social causes, but it remains true that the corporation must be able to claim that the element exists.

Indeed, satisfaction with the role of the corporation because it may come to reflect the attitudes of society would be premature, for firms have a special interest in the fastest possible rate of growth, which may not be compatible in the long run with the interests of society. We have seen that the corporation's profits depend essentially on economic growth and that any slowing down in the rate of increase in production tends to cut into the profits of the firm. The corporation must therefore press for policies that will cause the most rapid rate of growth. In addition, each particular company must be expected to try to manipulate opinion through advertising and promotion of all kinds so that the public will buy more of the goods it produces. If we should therefore decide that attempts to increase the rate of growth do not deserve the highest priority in coming years, we would need to re-examine the repercussions of the "governmental" nature of industry in the light of such a change in emphasis.

Another problem deserves some consideration. The directors of many companies represent essentially nobody but themselves. This lack of "legitimacy" of corporation control must be considered serious in the light of basic Western philosophy. The directors make their decisions in view of what they personally think is good for the company, and under normal circumstances no group can effectively question their decision. We have in fact the situation that Western philosophers have always dreaded, a group *with* power but *free* of social control. Such a situation has always been studiously avoided in government; its unexpected growth in business inevitably challenges many of the premises on which political theory is based.

"Power" in the company today lies with the director, but potential power is shifting once more. The amount of shares owned by other institutions rather than by individuals has been increasing rapidly. The most ardent collectors have been the pension, the insurance, and mutual funds. In the first two cases the collection of shares is a by-product of the main aim of the companies, which is to meet their future obligations to their policyholders or shareholders: they must invest in order to make their money yield sufficient to meet future commitments. The third type of company—the mutual funds—buy shares with money subscribed by investors who believe that the specialized management of these companies will make it possible to obtain a higher rate of interest or greater capital gains than they would obtain if they managed their own money.

Whether the purchase of shares is the direct business of the firm or merely a necessary by-product of the collection of money through pension and insurance funds, the result is that the voting rights of the shares thus purchased are vested in a company. The directors of these ownership companies must decide whether the ownership of shares should be considered as only conveying the right to an income, whether they should vote but always for the existing management, or whether they should vote their shares according to their judgment and thus influence the policy of other companies. Up to the present time one of the first two alternatives has usually been adopted, but there is always the possibility of changes if the various types of funds consider this more advantageous. In any case, the possible change in voting patterns must lead us to reconsider the whole concept of shareholder control.

Our present conventional idea of government is just as much of a stereotype as our views about industry. It is based essentially on the combined economic and political theories of the nineteenth century, which presented the individual as the only important unit, whose actions—regulated by his self-interest—would necessarily result in the "greatest good of the greatest number." Once such a theory was accepted, the confining and controlling forces of government could only be considered harmful, for they would, by definition, interfere with the free decisions of individuals and thus make society less satisfactory. This nineteenth-century view has been deeply embedded in all Western thought, but it gained the highest degree of acceptance in America.

Because of the concept of the legislator as an arbitrator between opposing individuals, a concept that emerges clearly from these theories, we periodically accord all the members of the population a chance to confirm the mandate of the legislator. We argue that, as the job of the legislator is to arbitrate the desires of various individuals, he will and should be re-elected if he has pleased the majority of the electorate; otherwise somebody else should take his place. The meaningfulness of this procedure in a complex world has been challenged on many grounds, notably that a decision to vote for or against a candidate cannot be significant, for it does not allow people to express their feelings about the policies that should be followed. They can only give a blanket endorsement or rejection to everything a candidate has done.

There is, however, a far more serious charge against the present system of voting—that the voter has no effective choice at all. It is the basic assumption of Western democratic thought that there will be at least two policies between which the voter can meaningfully choose—that he can choose a candidate who will support the policies he considers best. There have been many suggestions in recent years that this assumption is no longer valid—that whatever party is in power can only make minor changes in policies that are forced on it by outside events. If this is true, we must seek new justification for "democracy"; in these circumstances the voter cannot change or make policy; he decides on the party in power but not on the policy it follows.

It has generally been accepted by political scientists that the policies of the Democratic and Republican parties in America are not very different. In England there were clearly different parties until 1952—the Labour Party supported greater "social justice" and the Conservative Party supported "free enterprise." However, the policies of both parties in the last election were effectively identical. The Conservatives had contrived to obtain the credit for the policies that had been developed by the Labour Party. Similar evolutions have been taking place in other parts of the world.

Two changes have limited the possibility of the development of strongly differing programs for political parties in any country. The first is an increasing knowledge of the limitations of political, social, and economic action. It has been realized both by politicians and voters that some of the more utopian suggestions cannot be carried out, at least immediately. On the other hand, it has been seen that some new social policies *must* be adopted whether they agree with the official philosophy or not.

The second change has received more attention. Government is no longer primarily concerned with arbitrating between individuals, but with deciding on proper policies in a world where pressure groups agitate for the adoption of the views supported by the institutions they represent. These pressure groups operate on both parties—they try to gain support for their goals from both sides. In an occasional paper written by Arthur S. Miller for the Center for Democratic Institutions, entitled "Private Governments and the Constitution," the point is made in the following way: "The formation and establishment of important policies in the United States appear to require the reaching of a consensus among the groups most affected, beneficially or adversely, by these policies. As a result, policies tend to become those sanctioned by the lowest common denominator among interest groups, those that strike a balance between pleasing the most people and offending the fewest."

If this argument is valid, we are forced to reconsider the assumptions behind the periodical voting in Western countries. The accepted philosophy is that each member of the public, above a certain age, is given the right and privilege to decide on the policies he wants carried out. If, however, the policies the two parties propose are substantially similar, this privilege becomes more or less meaningless. But, although the procedure may be meaningless for the citizen, it remains essential for the legislator—unless he can preserve the support of his voters, he will fail to be re-elected. In many cases he will therefore be forced to compromise his principles in order to build a record and to retain the support of his party organization. As both parties often have the same aims and must accept the same limitations, he will have to spend much of his time trying to obtain the credit for actions that were possible and desired and to avoid the blame for those that were necessary but unpopular. The politician must try to put over an "image," a picture of his character. The scope of this revolution can be best appreciated if we try to imagine Lincoln or Washington dickering over the "image" they would present. It is the lack of real freedom to follow sharply differentiated policies that forces politicians to resort to lesser distinctions.

Why is it necessary to raise such a touchy subject? At first sight it might well appear that, as there is some value in individual voting and as there is no "practical" possibility of changing the system, it would be better to leave the subject alone. However, this argument is not valid. The generalized acceptance of existing methods as the best is dangerous, for it enables us to claim that the individual has adequate control over his government at the present time: we do not look for better methods that would be more suitable in today's conditions. The actual position is almost the opposite. There is considerable concern among political scientists that, unless certain existing trends are controlled, the collective—whether government or firm—will gain more and more power over the individual. Only if we recognize the unsatisfactory nature of our present system will we search for possible changes that will lead to a more satisfactory one.

What can we do to preserve the freedom of the individual in this situation? We must recognize that, despite the "forms" of individual voting, policies today are largely decided by pressure groups, and we must thereafter consider altering methods of individual control to take account of this fact. It seems to be generally believed that this is impossible—that there can be no prospect of changing Western governmental systems at the present time. The strength with which this idea is held is enhanced by the fact that one would not only need to alter the system of government but would also have to attack the philosophical underpinnings of the whole Western pattern of thought, which rest on the belief that the selfish actions of each person will maximize the welfare of the community. It is this doctrine that allows the manufacturer and the labor leader, the doctors and the farmer to press for the adoption of their own special interests with a clear conscience; they feel that their actions will necessarily be transmuted into good by the mysterious alchemy of the price mechanism. If we are to work out what is really best for the country and carry it through, we will require the support of all men of good will, for inertia and vested interests will interfere with the program. Under these circumstances we can hardly afford a political party whose duty it is to oppose for the sake of opposition rather than from a sense of conviction.

A perusal of the newspapers over even a limited period of time is sufficient to convince one of the growing challenge to the relevance of the political party. Many of the major reform programs in cities have been carried out by bipartisan groups rather than by conflicting political parties. There is increasing pressure to entrust the most important decisions or discussions to non-political organizations or to ensure balanced political membership of bodies set up to direct action. We are finding it increasingly necessary to accept the idea of a bipartisan foreign policy.

The governmental system of the West has been based on the belief that "truth" and "justice" would emerge from conflict.

This has always been a policy of the second-best; we have felt that man could not be trusted unless he was kept under close control. We have given up rapidity of action for greater certainty that action will not be self-seeking. Perhaps we must try a new idea—we must demand that man should become responsible and willing to make decisions on the basis of the general interest of the community. The problems that confront us are so great we will have to minimize unnecessary opportunities for dissension if we are to have any chance of success in the years ahead. The latter half of the twentieth century will demand great changes if we are to survive. Violence has been required in the past to accomplish changes of this magnitude—the ruling classes and vested interests were unwilling to alter conditions fast enough to avoid revolution.

Our whole philosophy is based on the right of each individual to strive to attain his own selfish goals: because of our basic philosophic structure we believe that clashes between private interests will be transmuted into the common good. Few individuals, and even fewer organizations, feel an obligation to examine the effects of their actions on the whole community: they consider their actions from the limited viewpoint of their own advantage.

Some change is, of course, already taking place in this area. The latest elections in all the Western countries have been fought to a far greater extent on global, rather than local, issues. The legislative process, however, has not kept up in most countries with this change in conditions. When legislation is being considered, each pressure group continues to lobby for its own interests, even when it knows that they will be detrimental to the community or the world as a whole. We must develop a system where discussion would be directed toward trying to discover the best policy for all and not for just the members of a particular group. Each person and each pressure group would be willing to concede that the interests of the community as a whole—*once they were known* —should take priority over their own interests.

This idea is deeply alien to the beliefs of the West. We have identified good government with the process of conflict between groups. We have forgotten that the requirement for counterbalancing power was set up, not as an ideal, but as a safeguard against abuse of power. The core of the argument is therefore simple. The world is enjoying or suffering from a scientific and economic revolution. This is changing our needs so rapidly as to demand very major alterations in ideas and policies that cannot be attained within our present concepts. The only possibility that seems adequate to the magnitude of the problem is that we should limit the degree of conflict and the use of power in decision-making and seek to work toward a general consensus. This in turn demands that man cease to fragment himself and try to examine the over-all issues. Our policy-making would still not be perfect, for we do not have sufficient knowledge or wisdom to discover the common good with certainty; but we would be hampered only by our ignorance and not by the fact that we do not admit the priority of the common good over private interest.

This suggestion may seem too drastic for many, but it is based on the fact that not even the most optimistic could suggest that the changes in social organization in the years since the war have kept pace with changing needs either nationally or internationally. Our failure to act has resulted in large part from a failure of understanding, but much of it also stems from the unwillingness of particular groups to see their position undermined and their profits undercut. We must find ways of compensating for change so that institutions and people will not suffer unduly—but more importantly we must find ways of negating the philosophy that claims that the right policy can, and indeed inevitably will, emerge from a conflict of selfishness.

All this is undoubtedly utopian and for that reason unrealistic to many. We are asking that man become unselfish. This is not necessarily impossible. "Selfishness" stems, at least in part, from the fact that Western economic and social systems are set up to encourage individualism. If we reduce the necessity for economic conflict, it may be that we can develop a co-operative form of society.

What goals should an abundant society accept? This is the final question we discuss in this part of the book, which has examined the challenge of abundance in the rich countries.

# 10.

## Our Goals in Tomorrow's World

THE LAST DECADE has seen the beginning of a groping search for a "national purpose" that would be adequate to meet the opportunities and challenges of the second half of the twentieth century. The need to discover new goals should not surprise us, for the Western countries have largely succeeded in fulfilling their primary task of the last hundred years—the attainment of a decent standard of living for all. What is surprising and hopeful is that attention has been concentrated in recent months on this lack of a clear goal for the future and that people have been discussing the goals to which the Western nations should now aspire.

Only the "queen of the academic disciplines," philosophy, can hope to give us the answers to the questions we now face. Philosophy's royal title, however, has always been somewhat empty. The daily obligations of the greater part of mankind have been too pressing for most people to be able to pay attention to the theoretical prescriptions developed by philosophers. In addition, lack of knowledge of the learning process and the way in which societies were organized made it impossible to apply the proposals made by philosophers. Within the lifetime of this generation we will have the leisure to listen to the philosopher and the knowledge that will permit us to change man deliberately. Indeed the knowledge we are gaining about methods of learning, about biology, and about the process of decision-making—both human and machine—makes it essential that we know what to do, for otherwise we will merely accept passively the steps that scientists make possible.

We must reconsider what we mean by the phrases "the right to life, liberty and the pursuit of happiness" and the French *"Liberté, Fraternité, Egalité."* What real meaning can they have in the acutely interdependent modern world? They lead to a series of questions, each of them more unanswerable than the one before it. What is liberty? What is equality? How do we reconcile liberty and equality? What is happiness? Can one pursue happiness, or will it inevitably escape as one moves toward it? We can transmute these into more practical but still-unanswered questions. How should the distribution of income be arranged in a society of abundance? How do we make sure that people are not injured by actions that enable others to gain additional profits? How do we make certain that the desire for equal education for all does not damage the educational opportunities for the most intelligent? What is education and what is propaganda? Would eugenics be right or justifiable?

At the present time we are allowing science to change man's outlook on life, without examining whether the results should be encouraged or not. David Lilienthal suggests that science

will inevitably affect man's thinking and this appears beneficial to him. "By the time the 21st Century opens its doors science and scientists can, and I believe will, have profoundly
influenced and shaped the mind of man, his outlook on life,
his attitude toward his neighbors in the next block and across
the seas, his understanding of himself as an individual. . . .

"The traditional forces and institutions that for centuries
have so nobly affected and shaped men's ideas and ideals need
reinforcing—need it critically. Among these are the law, the
arts, religion, diplomacy, education."

A slight development of the idea shows how this approach
can lead to considering man as nothing more than an auto-
maton to be eventually replaced by machines. Dr. Edward
Teller said at a UNESCO conference on computers: "If we
give the machine a large enough memory and give it enough
random trials, it will remember those trials which are successful. It will thus learn. I believe that the machine can be
given the power to make value judgments as well as logical
reasoning, and that from that I can construct, mathemati-
cally, a model for machine emotion. . . . When you come
down to it, what is the difference between machine-thinking
and your own thinking? We cannot draw the line. Any human process which is logical can be copied by the machine."

We must ask further questions. Do we want or need the
ever-increasing standard of living that the wondrous system
we have constructed will automatically provide? We have set
the sorcerer's apprentice to work. The corporation requires
change and exists because of change. Its survival in its present
form, therefore, depends on the destruction of the old and its
replacement by the new. Are we, as a society, ready for an
ever-increasing standard of living and a steadily falling number of hours at work? Above all, do we know how to deal with
the revolution that will result by the year 2000 if we use our

ability to multiply our standard of living by a factor of three or four, and decrease our hours of work to the same extent?

So deeply rooted are past ideas that demanded a further increase in income that questioning this approach is still unfashionable except in certain very limited circles. The reluctance to approach this problem is enhanced by the fact that we are all aware that our personal standard of living and that of most of our friends is too low and that we could all use about 25 to 50 per cent more income than we actually have. But this is somewhat irrelevant, for we will always need additional money as long as we believe that our most important aim is to raise the material standard of living. Man's needs *can* be insatiable.

It is difficult to accept that our income could be sufficient and that our feeling that we do not have enough comes from our failure to use the available resources well, rather than from our need for more. We look on all goods as scarce and therefore try to increase our consumption, believing that abundance will solve our difficulties. David Riesman has made a balanced statement of the problems in the *Bulletin of the Atomic Scientists:* "The age of abundance has its grandeurs and its miseries which are both like and unlike those of any other age, and the searching of aims and discovery of motives appropriate to our new forms of peril and opportunity, along with the discovery of ways to institutionalize our collective inspirations, seems to me the fundamental economic and meta-economic task."

We prefer not to admit that abundance brings new miseries: we want to believe that abundance will relieve us of all problems and dangers not only of the past but in the future. This view can be destroyed by examining one issue that perhaps comprises all the others. Abundance will eliminate many of the challenges that were of prime importance before its coming. This change is final and definitive: we cannot continue to pretend that we need to allow people to starve and suffer from disease in order to spur others to activity. Our ancient and basic challenge of providing enough goods to sustain life is disappearing.

But we will not reach the millennium, as some had hoped. Other miseries and annoyances are taking the place of those which have vanished. We need only look at two of them. The first is the prevalence of shoddy work, the almost nonexistent pleasure in a job well done. Many commercial firms no longer suffer greatly from this policy, for it is more trouble for the customer to take cheap things back than to throw them away. "It will do" is the motto, and we can replace it when it goes wrong. An economy of abundance is under present rules also an economy of waste and repetition—indeed without this waste the economy would slump. Nobody, however, can be optimistic about the survival of a society with such values.

The other "misery" stems from the first, although the causal connection between the two is only now being recognized. There are too few people who have anything important to do with their time. It is not necessary that the "important" thing for one person should seem vital or even interesting to others as long as it provides a clue to the reason for existence and gives a man something worth while to do. In the absence of a valued occupation or hobby too many people are bored. In *Mirage of Health,* Dr. René Dubos says: "[Boredom] often masquerades in the passive forms of entertainment, in the dreary hours of aimless driving, in anonymous holidays which have lost their meaning because they are no longer holy, as well as in the attitude of the person who 'couldn't care less' about the events of the world around him." It also results in the delinquency of the child who takes risks or does damage that would not seem necessary to him if he had something to take himself out of himself.

The weakness of the Western world lies in our lack of involvement. The communists have faith in their system and are trying to remake the world in their own image. The discussed youths in our culture are not those with something positive to contribute, but the "angry young men" of England and the "beat generation" who are quite simply "anti." We fail to provide opportunities for those who *do* care: those who would like to effect events are unable to see how they can do so.

Too many feel trapped by a new orthodox philosophy we are told we must accept: that mankind forms part of a "process," that the scientific knowledge being developed will create a new world into which *man must fit*. In more extreme examples of this theory we are informed that if man does not use this new knowledge he will have "failed." The institutional economists have been one of the main developers of these theories; they have suggested that it is machinery that is important. Clarence Ayres put it this way: "It is this technological continuum which is the locus of truth and value." Peter Drucker, in his book *Landmarks of Tomorrow,* also came close to locating truth and value in the process of development. "By contrast we today no longer even understand the question whether change is in itself bad or good. We start out with the axiom that it is the norm. We do not see change as altering the order—for better or for worse. We see change as being order in itself—indeed the only order we can comprehend today is a dynamic, a moving, a changing one."

Mankind must control the process of development. We must decide what is important and learn how to preserve the meaning of life for each individual. De Tocqueville saw over a century ago a truth that has still not been generally recognized: "When the conditions of society are becoming more equal, and each individual man becomes more like all the rest, more weak and more insignificant, a habit grows up of ceasing to notice the citizens to consider only the people, and of overlooking the individuals to think only of their kind." The individual has been submerged within the various collectives to which he belongs: we have to find ways to free him from this bondage.

We can do this only if we develop new ideas and institutions that will work in the new situations. John Dewey put this need succinctly in *Freedom and Culture*. "A culture which permits science to destroy traditional values but which distrusts its power to create new ones is a culture which is destroying itself." What are the elements that are destroying our present culture patterns and what are the factors we must bear in mind as we try to develop a new value system or "sense of national purpose" appropriate for the age in which we live? First, we must accept the inevitability of the increase in production that will make it possible and indeed imperative to provide an adequate income for everybody. Second, we must realize the enormous scope of the revolution of rising knowledge that lies behind the increase in wealth, and we must accept the fact that we cannot arrest this revolution: we can only control the way the resulting information is used. Man must learn to live with this increase in knowledge.

One of the major problems we shall face is that biology will present us with the information that will allow us to "improve" the genetic make-up of the race. We shall be able to decide on the types of children we wish to have and to breed for these qualities as we now do in race horses. *Fortune* in a recent article posed the problem in the following terms: "Sooner or later, biology will inevitably present man with the means of altering—perhaps improving—his innate biological make-up. The social problems produced by such biological mastery would be staggering. Can man learn to handle the power to raise his intelligence, to double his life span, or to change the color of his skin? These capabilities may seem so remote as to scarcely be worth worrying about today. But just the modest capability of enabling parents to select the sex of their children, a possibility already foreshadowed in animal experiments, might throw society off balance in a dozen different ways. That biology will present society with vexatious problems of some sort, probably before the end of the century, is, to biologists, a foregone conclusion."

One example from a recent development will show the nature of the problems that can arise. The possibility of artificial insemination has already gravely shaken our views about the rights of wives and husbands and about legitimacy and illegitimacy. Other developments in prospect are far more startling. But this is not the most basic problem. The possibility of the biological improvement of mankind is far less important in determining man's potential than the views and values that prevail in each society. Our most immediate problem lies in our need to understand the process of education. We are only now beginning to accept that it will inevitably affect the views of each person throughout his life. We are only now beginning to accept that it is wishful thinking to assume that there are certain forms of education that imprint the mind of the child and others that do not. All training for life inculcates certain values, and this process is necessary if the child is to be able to take his place in society.

Just how unacceptable such an idea is at present was demonstrated most vividly in a television program on future developments in computers. The major question in the program was "Can Machines Think?" However, discussion of this question was hampered by the fact that it was considered necessary to spend a large part of the program explaining that the process of teaching a human being and that of feeding facts into a computer were not so very different. We will see at the end of the chapter that there is an essential difference between the machine brain and the human brain—however, this difference does not lie in the capacity to absorb knowledge and to take logical decisions.

We must change our attitude toward social phenomena just as we have already changed our attitude to scientific phenomena. In the Middle Ages the scientist who dared to follow his own judgment was castigated and even killed for his temerity in questioning the accepted view about the universe. We have now learned—to a great extent—to accept the description of scientific phenomena as factual and even nonemotional. We did not execute Einstein, although he revolutionized our universe: indeed, he even received a measure of fame for his work.

In the social sciences, however, our position is similar to that which existed in the physical sciences in the Middle Ages. Institutions are defended not because of their utility in a given situation but because the emotional security of an individual or a society is bound up in them. Our views about the private-enterprise system are not based—as we would like to believe—on a hardheaded examination of the advantages and disadvantages of the system; they result from an emotional commitment to the free-enterprise system. Our loyalty to present methods of labor-management bargaining is based not on its proven ability to cope with present conditions but on its past history. Unless we can learn to accept the need for change in methods of controlling society, we will be unable to produce a viable way of life for today's world.

Such a viable society will require a greater degree of unselfishness and love than has yet been achieved by human beings. Man has always been largely controlled by arbitrary shibboleths derived from past events. He has obeyed the magical and social taboos laid down for his control, and has accepted these restraints. Western man is no longer willing to do so: indeed their sacrosanct nature could not survive unquestioned in a "rational" age. We have now to develop new systems that will allow men to live together in society: if freedom is to be secured, these systems will depend more on the initiative of the individual himself and less on the group. The degree of control exerted by society over the individual has been decreasing in the rich countries for a long period. Unfortunately, the power of the individual to develop a system of values for himself has not kept pace. Many people feel that they no longer have any rules that will suffice to guide their lives.

This brings us face to face with a question already mentioned. What is the real and fundamental meaning of freedom? This is a question that has engaged philosophers throughout the centuries, and I do not pretend to be able to answer it fully here. But we cannot discuss the goals for the rich countries without examining the most fundamental of all—that of meaningful freedom for everybody.

Our easiest task is to dispose of the widespread assumption that freedom can be equated with license. It is still too often simply assumed that freedom involves the right to do whatever one wishes regardless of its effects on others. Freedom is not license—it is the right to take a stand for what one believes to be right against what one thinks is wrong. *Freedom is the possibility to make meaningful choices.* Freedom exists, therefore, when the individual can make a reasoned choice between a number of possible courses of action. In order to do this he has both to understand the factors that should influence his decision and the consequences likely to stem from it.

There is another condition for the existence of real freedom: it is essential that dissent should not carry overwhelming penalties: that it should be possible for the man with a wife and children to stand up for an unpopular view without jeopardizing their future. Dissent from the accepted view will of course always be unpopular and therefore carry some penalties, for the dissenter will wish to destroy established positions and damage the interests of others. We can only try to make sure that the cost of dissent is not so high as to be impossible for the vast majority of people.

We must realize that freedom involves a series of basic and classic paradoxes. We have tended to believe that the person without values was free; we are only now discovering that the man without any goals cannot direct his life. Our misunderstanding of this fact has also tended to confuse us, as we have tried to compare the position of the person in the underdeveloped country or primitive tribe with our own position today. We have suggested that, because the lives of those in the underdeveloped countries were bound by a tight set of cultural imperatives, they had little or no freedom. We make the fundamental error of trying to put ourselves in their place and, as we would be unbearably restricted by the norms of such a society, we claim that they can have had no freedom of action. Yet we must realize that they felt free, they stood erect, and believed that they lived full lives.

This question of meaningful freedom is the great philosophic and human problem of our age. We know that society exists because of shared values—whether they be as simple as the right hour to arrive at a cocktail party or as complex as the pattern of rights and duties of each member of the community. We no longer know how society should obtain a commitment from all its members to these necessary standards, nor do we know what are the minimum shared values required for the survival of a society. We do know that certain suggestions made proposing the abolition of all shared values are unrealistic: the only relevant question is what and how many shared values there should be and how they should be developed. Man *must* live by a set of values: without some values life becomes meaningless. If we fail to develop valid goals for the members of society—goals found to be meaningful and attainable—any rabble rouser who can orate will be able to take over the society.

We would do well to listen to the views of Africa. Julius Nyerere put it this way in an article in *The New York Times Magazine:* "The West seems to have exaggerated its idea of freedom beyond the point where freedom becomes license; to have accepted a society, in which, provided a man does not too obviously steal or murder, he can defend any form of self-indulgence by calling it 'freedom of the individual.' The Communist world—largely, I think, as a reaction against this exaggeration—has swung like a pendulum to the other extreme; the individual in a Communist society is secondary to something called the state.

"Here, then, I think, is the problem: where does society, or the state, draw the boundary of its rights and obligations; and where does the individual? It is a problem that has not yet been solved by either side in a way that can be accepted by the other."

We have found to our dismay that the West's attempt to throw off the "limiting" effect of cultural imperatives has only too often backfired. We have challenged people to decide for themselves how they would live: we have removed most of the absolute rules that regulated conduct in the past. But the results have not been what we had hoped to obtain. There would be fairly general agreement that this process has often led, not to increased independence, but to a deadening pattern of conformity. Why did this happen? Today few people feel that their own personal values are sufficiently well grounded to uphold them against the opposition of the groups within which they may live. Indeed, in some cases they have so few values of their own they are perfectly willing to accept all the views of a society in order to guarantee their acceptance within it.

Thus in the suburbs many wives feel bound to form part of the suburban kaffee-klatsch and to be involved in a variety of "accepted" good works—even if they believe that other ways of spending their time would be more useful. These suburban areas usually have a general consensus about the "right" standard of living, and society is organized in such a way that both those who fall below this level and those who move far ahead of it feel acutely uncomfortable.

An even greater problem faces the executive in the corporation. A man's career depends on his ability to make his superiors think that he is the best person for promotion. Whether rightly or wrongly, he often feels that he will get ahead only if he minimizes his conflicts with the views of his superiors—both in terms of policies and ethics. Many people fear that the corporation is therefore coming to dictate the "moral" judgment of its executives, that once the company has defined a certain set of actions as "right" most executives will not feel it necessary or possible to challenge these views. Morality, however, cannot be a corporate responsibility, for the corporation will inevitably tend to accept and even define as right anything necessary for its survival. We have seen that business requires the most rapid possible rate of growth if it is to obtain satisfactory profits. Its "morality" will inevitably tend to be "permissive" in any area where prospects of growth are involved. Thus we see business reluctant to challenge some of the more doubtful ethics of the advertising field on the implicit or explicit ground that they are essential to the survival of the free-enterprise system. We must not allow one interest in society to control its members completely when there is a potential danger that the policies of the partial group and those of the total society may clash.

The resulting trend toward conformity may be sincerely deplored by many. But each aspiring executive knows that his whole future depends on the "total" judgment his superiors have of his abilities and his character. He is therefore unwilling to risk deviant behavior that may jeopardize his chances of future promotion.

Attention has been largely concentrated on the more obvious pressures on both the firm and the individual that tend to lead to conformity—for example, the fact that many personality tests weed out any extreme personalities—a fact that William Whyte, in his book *The Organization Man,* proposed countering by the developing of a synthetic personality for the purpose of the test. There are other, less obvious forces also working to make it almost impossible for the firm to risk the employment of an individual who may affect the company's image by a strong and unauthorized action.

However, the firm is also subject to outside pressures that tend to lead to the encouragement of conformity. It is well known by now that many firms require that all writings by members of their staff should be "cleared" by the company. One firm imposed this requirement after it had been asked by the government to explain the published views of one of the junior members of its staff and had to send a substantial portion of its legal personnel to Washington to deal with the issue. It is not surprising that the company decided it could not afford to risk any possible duplication of this event.

The potential results of these pressures toward conformity were graphically demonstrated in *The Organization Man* and from a slightly different angle in *Life in the Crystal Palace*. These and the many other books on the subject all illustrate the fact that one of the basic conditions of freedom is not fulfilled for the individual who works in the corporation today. The dissenter fears that his possibility of success and indeed his chance of any form of satisfactory career may be destroyed if he disagrees with the accepted norms. While this fear may sometimes be exaggerated, it is sufficiently realistic to make it necessary to consider the ways in which dissent may be made less damaging.

To suggest that those living in Western society today may be less free to disagree than those who lived in past centuries is to court ridicule or even worse. And yet our societies tolerate and make possible less divergence from their norms than many earlier cultures. Our social system demands such a high standard of material wealth that most men must work, and, as work normally requires set hours, man has little freedom to organize his life as he wishes. The conventional justification for this is interesting. We claim that the discipline of work is good. As a result our society attaches a strong stigma to idleness and few can afford to accept the consequences of this choice. While this system may possibly be beneficial, it can hardly be described as freedom.

It can be argued that despite this fact the degree of freedom is greater today than ever before. But the argument fails to convince completely for two reasons. First, many earlier societies achieved a far more flexible use of time than the West has today. Indeed, difficult as it may be for the West to accept this point, many societies made no distinction between work and leisure and indeed had no words for them. They considered life as an over-all pattern—all of which was valuable. Second, our society has less satisfactory arrangements to free those who are able to think and create than many poorer societies. We claim that we can allow the market place to judge whether an artist or a writer, a philosopher or a thinker should spend his time in such pursuits. The development of a society of abundance will allow us to extend the area of freedom by accepting an obligation to provide a minimum standard of living for all the members of society without dictating the task they should perform.

Just as the development of economic abundance could allow us to increase the range of freedom, so too the rapidly increasing range of knowledge could be used to increase freedom. But there is a danger that it may actually have precisely the opposite result. As we have already seen, freedom is meaningful only when we *understand* the forces that affect our lives and *comprehend* the outcome of the various choices we make. The present economic and scientific revolutions are rapidly destroying the relevance of old theories, but we are not informing people of the meaning or effects of these changes. As a result, we are forcing many people to abdicate their decision-making function: they find it necessary to accept the ideas of those who claim that they understand the problems. Many other people are basing their decisions on inadequate or faulty information.

The expressed desire of the West is to increase man's control over the environment and thus increase the range of choices open to him. But we have hardly discussed the pressing danger that the growth of knowledge may prevent the individual from controlling his own life. It seems eminently possible that continuation of present trends will force the individual to abdicate effective control to a dictatorial group or, implicitly, to computers. We have lost sight of our basic goals. Science and economics have been driving us for centuries to consider primarily the factual and the quantifiable. We ignore the emotions; we have forgotten that it is the emotions that make us human. We refuse to recognize that without them we might as well be robots—indeed, we would be robots.

It is the failure to understand this fact and the suggestion that man's decisions can be replaced by machine decisions that is one of the most frightening and potentially dangerous of all the developments that assail us today. This danger goes far deeper than the old and much-examined fear that the machine may dehumanize us: there is a real possibility that we may allow the machine to take over and control our destiny. Norbert Wiener explained in the following passage how this could occur: "As is now generally admitted, over a limited range of operation, machines act far more rapidly than human beings. . . . This means that though machines are theoretically subject to human criticism, such criticism may be ineffective until long after it is relevant. To be effective in warding off disastrous consequences, our understanding of our man-made machines should, in general, develop *pari-passu* with the performance of the machine. By the very slowness of our human actions, our effective control of our machines may be nullified. By the time we are able to react to information conveyed by our senses and stop the car we are driving, it may already have run head-on into a wall."

Man must be left the right to choose. It is choice and the emotions that separate man from machines; these emotions are remarkably inefficient and irrational, but they are essential to our humanity. One of the most pleasing demonstrations of the distinction between humanity and rationality occurred on the occasion of the opening of the Seagram Building in New York. In order to celebrate the occasion it was decided to hold a symposium on "The Future of Man." Blessed perhaps with a deep appreciation of the problems of mankind or, possibly, with a mere sense of the need for contrast, the speakers included not only the representatives of the scientific disciplines that are trying to perceive order in life but also Robert Frost, a representative of the poets, whose existence depends upon the unexpected and the ironical. The report not only contains statements about the need for increasing understanding of the world and of the human being; it also stresses that, if we succeed in removing all the illogicalities from human existence, we will destroy mankind.

Let me quote from Robert Frost's brief speech:

"Next are we going to be another kind of people? Young people of our day, in studying anthropology and listening to the anthropologists, think it's such an amusing distance between the monkeys and us, that it will be only another amusing distance from us to the superman. . . . Let me tell you about that—I know just what's going to happen or not happen. Our self-consciousness is terminal—there's nothing beyond us. Life in us has reached a self-consciousness that terminates the growth."

Mankind must take decisions about its future course. Assuming that we avoid the holocaust of a nuclear war—for it is only this assumption that makes prediction of any kind worth while—a hundred years will allow us to produce a reasonable standard of living for all those on earth. Long before this time we will face the challenge of what our ultimate goal must be. In one of his last publications before his death, Robert Redfield wrote a conversation between a stranger who seemed to have come from another planet and himself. The stranger asked the following question, which perhaps poses in all its acuteness the dilemma that confronts us. ". . . To take risks, make adventures, create and add to human life, is it necessary to climb a mountain or build a spaceship, or could we also adventure and create within a limited world? Find new good things within the limits of earth-space, production

and consumption? Exercise restraints to free one's self for
the making of new things for enjoyment, improved experience, wiser and finer judgments. Where is freedom? In always doing more and more or in doing fewer things to do
them better? That, of course, amounts to asking if the very
abundance of material goods may not result in a loss of
freedom."

**PART III**

*The International Challenge*

# 11.

## *The Needs of the Poor Countries*

IT IS HARDLY POSSIBLE to summarize the conclusions of the previous chapters in a few sentences, but we can probably agree that the most important development in the rich countries in the twentieth century is that the improvement in the standard of education and the increase in the quantity of material resources have greatly increased the *potential* for freedom. However, we have seen that the mere existence of greater opportunities for freedom does not guarantee that they will be seized. Many would agree that the population and even the leaders of the rich countries have been shying away from the issues that have been raised by the increasing freedom of choice. At the very beginning of our examination of the future course of the poor countries we must understand and accept the incontrovertible fact that the *absence* of a large educated class and of sufficient material resources deprives the poor countries of this freedom. Their possible range of actions is very narrowly circumscribed by the fact that they must concentrate on satisfying the minimal demands of their populations for a better life.

Such an idea will be extremely unpopular in the Western world. We like to believe that we can apply the concepts of "right" and "wrong" to all the actions of the poor countries: we are loath to admit that political, social, and economic conditions can force a certain pattern of reactions. Tom Mboya took the West to task for this tendency, charging that the West expected from the poor countries standards of conduct it had not yet been able to attain for itself. "If honest mistakes are made, we should not be apologetic, for this is part of the process of operating a democracy the world over. It is ironic—and indeed, flattering—that the older powers should ask us to guarantee perfection when they have not, even after hundreds of years, reached perfection themselves."

Our failure of comprehension in this field, as in so many others, stems from the fact that we do not examine all the implications of an accepted idea. It has become almost a cliché to say that it is the increased material welfare and education of the rich countries that have increased their possible range of action. If this is true, a mere reversal of the argument will show that the absence of these two favorable developments in the poor countries of the world prevents them from attaining the degree of freedom now available in the rich. The poor countries will be constrained to certain actions because of their need for economic growth, while the lack of economic sophistication of their populations will often force their leaders to take steps they would wish to avoid. It is this line of reasoning that leads directly to the "self-preservation" argument for the importance of foreign aid. Foreign aid increases the quantity of material resources available to the leaders of the poor countries and thus increases their possible range of actions. This may enable them to avoid adopting policies that are necessary because they help their country in the short run but that incidentally damage the interests of the rich.

Whatever the amount of help given by the rich countries, we must not expect that the policies of the poor countries will inevitably and continuously coincide with the interests of the rich. Too often in the past the rich countries have reacted as though the poor were not only damaging the interests of the developed, when they suggested or made changes in economic, political, and social organization, but were also upsetting an *inviolate* social order. The rich countries must realize that the needs of the poor will not always coincide with their own and that we can no longer assume that the differences can always be composed on the basis of the old social and economic order laid down by the rich.

However, it will not be enough to develop an "understanding" attitude toward the actions of the poor countries. Many idealists have suggested that a change of heart in the rich countries of the world would be sufficient to solve all problems. They argue that, if the rich countries would only lend enough capital and make enough technicians available, no other steps would be needed; at the very least they suggest that all other difficulties would become of peripheral importance. It is the object of this chapter to suggest that there are, in fact, very strict limits to the rate of increase in the amount of money that can be absorbed by the poor countries of the world, that education—in its broadest sense—is the most basic need if *real* and *lasting* progress is to be made, and that the first need for valid education is not more money but an understanding of the dimensions of the problem.

The first necessity is to bring into focus the real difference between the standard of living in the rich and the poor countries of the world. The usually quoted figures that show that the income per head of the United States is some twenty-five times greater than that of some of the poor countries are extremely misleading. Present statistical methods do not allow a meaningful comparison of the standard of living of America and India, of the United Kingdom and Japan. The standards of different civilizations are so unlike that comparison on a quantitative basis is simply meaningless.

This simple denial of the relevance of conventional measurements does not dispose of the problem. Even though the gap between the standards of living of the rich and poor countries is not so wide as is generally suggested, it is known and accepted that there are considerable areas in the world where a large proportion of the population is permanently hungry, where life expectancy does not exceed forty years, and where chronic diseases are widespread. In such countries there is a need for a rapid increase in standards of living. However, the poor countries will be really successful only if they avoid the errors into which America and Russia have fallen, and that Western Europe now appears to be trying to emulate—the identification of human happiness and success with the ability to purchase large quantities of material goods. New standards of measurement must be developed that do not make it appear that a country is falling down on its job simply because it sometimes places the preservation of traditional values above the changes that would ensure continued economic growth.

Americans now enjoy a standard of living far above any ever achieved before. If one leaves aside the problem of maldistribution of wealth, it is clear that even those who have benefited most from this cornucopia have not been satisfied by the increase in their material standards. We have only succeeded in creating a climate of permanent dissatisfaction—

the great majority of the people in the rich countries always require 25 or 50 per cent more material goods than they have at the present time, and concentrate their energies on obtaining them. We inhabit the Red Queen's world, where we must run ever faster to stay in the same place. There are many who claim that satisfaction comes from seeking an attainable goal rather than one that constantly recedes before us, that we need the encouragement that comes from achievement. There is little evidence that the pursuit of an ever-rising standard of living is conducive to happiness.

The problem facing us is to decide how much emphasis the poor countries should lay on the need for economic growth, how drastically they should revise their social system to encourage economic growth. The most vital difference between the rich and poor countries is that the poor countries have not attached much importance to economic growth in the past and are not organized to encourage the changes required if they are to attain it. Economic growth in the Western countries, in Russia, and in Japan resulted from the dissolution and destruction of social patterns that limited the rate of change in response to economic forces. In America, where this process has gone furthest, the individual often moves his home every two or three years, leaving behind him all but his immediate family. This caused a major—if little noticed—revolution that separates the generation born around the turn of the century from those born between the two World Wars. The older generation typically knew every limb of its family tree, and can trace all the great-uncles and second cousins twice removed. To the younger generation this is slightly amusing or downright ridiculous: the family usually consists of husband, wife, and children. Some residual loyalty may remain for one's parents and perhaps for brothers and sisters, but this is the normal limit of interest.

Many people will go where their jobs take them—their

work is the controlling factor in their lives. If one line of industry declines, people are increasingly willing to enter another—they feel no emotional bond with their trade or even their profession. The concept of man as a unit of labor is still gaining ground simply because men have subordinated their social interests to their economic—we have made arrangements that allow men to be used "efficiently" and moved from one occupation to another with the minimum of difficulty.

It is obvious that this process of depersonalization is not complete. But the emotional tie between an individual and his profession or trade has declined. We have only to go back one century to see the extent of this change. One of the tragedies of the nineteenth century was the slow death of the profession of the hand-loom weaver in England. They were deprived of their occupation by the invention of power looms, but they did not leave their traditional field. Almost unbelievable suffering resulted from their continuance in a dying occupation. The failure to find new jobs stemmed from two radically different causes. First, the people were emotionally attached to their work and showed reluctance to leave it. Second, the employment "market" hardly existed; there were no efficient methods of moving people from one industry to another.

In most of the poor countries an emotional loyalty to a way of life continues. Unless we realize this difference between the present loyalty patterns of the rich and poor countries, intervention to cause more "efficient" production can lead to widespread misery and hardship. The people in the poor countries of the world are still generally attached to their trades and professions; their satisfaction is greatly decreased if they are forced to change from one type of employment to another. Moreover, in many areas of the poor countries there are no possibilities for change—the removal of one type of employment opportunity for any reason *automatically* deprives some people of work, for there is already considerable unemployment.

The disruptive economic effects of changes in the poor countries are greatly enhanced by the social effects. The prevailing social order in the poor countries is still kin-based or tribal-based. Movement from one place to another to seek work often destroys the moral and social supports through which man has lived. We continue to forget that economic growth is for people and that their lives should not be distorted to serve economic growth. Indeed, in the West we have so completely accepted the argument that economic behavior does not involve values that we have forgotten that it is capable of arousing great emotional reactions. Karl Polanyi in *Trade and Market in the Early Empires,* calls our attention to this:"". . . only in the presence of a system of price-making markets will exchange acts of individuals result in fluctuating prices that integrate the economy. Otherwise such acts of barter will remain ineffective and therefore tend not to occur. Should they nevertheless happen, in a random fashion, a violent emotional reaction would set in, as against acts of indecency or acts of treason, since trading behavior is never emotionally indifferent behavior and is not, therefore, tolerated by opinion outside of the approved channels."

The West wants the people of the poor countries to live as we do ourselves. We pity the nomad who is clearly "poverty-stricken." We fail to understand that his life can be more richly satisfying than our own. The Iranian Government has attempted to encourage many of the migratory tribes to settle in recent years. For a complex of economic, social, and spiritual reasons the result was sometimes the destruction of the way of life, the health, and even the limited economic wealth of the tribe.

In our desire to improve the material condition of the world we are forgetting that the standard of living is not an end in itself but a means. We analyze societies to see whether they are capable of rapid economic growth, rather than examining them in order to see how the necessary economic growth can be used to preserve the values of these countries. We fail to realize that man can understand life only if his values allow him to comprehend the situation. Our plans often do not take account of the fact that, although the human mind has great capacities for adjustment, it can easily be overloaded, and overloading it can lead to mental stress or even mental breakdown. We are only now beginning to understand that the result of such overstrain may be irrational and inexplicable behavior; that people trapped in situations they find too difficult of solution may become childlike or may return to old forms of behavior they had previously abandoned. Only if people "understand" situations in the fullest sense will they be able to make sensible decisions.

One of the major limits to any realistic program for improving conditions in the poor countries must therefore be in terms of the ability of the society and the individual to accept change. In addition, any program must also recognize that many of the present reactions in the poor countries are unfavorable to economic growth. These behavior patterns lead to the "vicious circle" analysis, which is basic to economic development theory. It is correctly argued that unless we can find ways to change certain reactions much of the money contributed by the Western countries cannot be successfully used.

The vicious circle most often examined is the increase in population that usually follows any increase in production and income. None of the poor countries has a really effective birth-control program; population increase has been limited in the past by the death of the majority of children before they reached adulthood. The death of children resulted from two different causes; first, the extremely poor health conditions in most countries and, second, the fact that famines occurred periodically following failures in harvests, and this led to large increases in the death rate.

Both these forces, which kept the rate of population increase low in earlier centuries, are now being limited in their effects. In the years since World War II each country has tried to reduce the toll of disease; the work of the World Health Organization has had dramatic results in reducing the incidence of malaria and other diseases. Also, few famines have developed, emergency exports of grains from those countries with surplus stocks being made whenever a dearth threatened. As a result of these changes death rates have declined throughout the world and the number of people in many poor countries has risen rapidly. In far too many countries the rise in population has taken up *all* the available increase in production; none of it has been available to *raise* standards of living.

A second type of vicious circle results from the increasing importance of consumer goods in almost all countries of the world. It is generally agreed that growth can be attained only if part of the resources of a country is devoted to investment —to the production of dams, factories, machinery, which will increase production in future years. The "revolution of rising expectations" is continually cutting into the resources available for investment and thus the rate of growth.

This vicious circle is inevitable in a world divided into two types of countries—the rich and the poor; the poor countries wish to attain the standards of the rich before it is possible for them to do so. However, the actions of both the rich and the poor countries have greatly increased the force behind the "revolution of rising expectations." The rich countries have done their best to bring their higher standard of living to the attention of the inhabitants of the poor in the years since the war. The result, in all too many cases, has been to build up resentment. In addition, the governments of the poor countries have themselves encouraged the trend toward a desire for greater consumption. Advertising, which must inevitably increase felt wants, is allowed; some governments have introduced commercial television and some have even permitted time-payment plans that allow consumers to buy goods before they have money available. In the poor countries where the overwhelming problem is a shortage of resources, such steps can only be unfavorable and act to reduce the rate of economic growth.

The third—and almost certainly least-understood—vicious circle depends on the relation between the income the individual receives and the amount he is willing to do. If the price a producer gets for his goods doubles, he needs to do only about half the amount of work to obtain the same standard of living. Under these circumstances what should he do? What would be his rational course of action? This depends on what his goal in life may be. If he has fixed wants, and has no desire to work for its own sake, he will decrease the amount of time he spends producing goods. This reaction has plagued those from the Western countries for many decades; they have tended to call this reaction "laziness." In many cases wage increases have had to be reversed because they decreased the amount of work people were willing to do.

We have not been much concerned with this problem of laziness in Western countries in the twentieth century, for those who do not work are looked upon askance, and a continuing increase in consumption is generally accepted. Social prestige in the Western countries demands that one have a job. A humorous plot for a highly successful television play will illustrate this better than any argument. The story turned on the fact that the husband liked housework and the wife liked to go out to work. They therefore resolved to change their roles—the husband would cease to work in an office while the wife would take a job. This unorthodox division of labor was heartily despised by the neighbors. The resulting problems were solved only when the wife arranged for the publication of one of *her* manuscripts under her *husband's* name. It was then accepted that he was respectably employed writing—he was not "idling." However, we must remember that the evolution of these attitudes is recent. As late as the mid-nineteenth century the complaint was general that the result of higher wages was not more but less labor, not a better but an inferior standard of work. The laborer was only too willing to quit his job and get drunk for a portion of the week if his wages permitted it.

Although work is usually considered necessary in the rich countries, it is often less acceptable in the poor. One particular facet of this reaction is particularly serious for the possibilities of economic development. Not only do employees tend to quit their work when they have obtained the amount of money they feel they need; those in charge of firms react in the same way. The entrepreneur, the person who causes economic growth by making changes that lead to greater efficiency in the economic system, tends to do less work if his income increases. Unlike the employer or director of firms in Western countries, his prestige is not tied up with the economic growth of his firm. Robert Heilbroner, in *The Quest for Wealth,* pointed up the difference between the businessman in North and South America. ". . . what is it which drives the American businessman so relentlessly when his easier-going Latin counterpart has long ago retired? What is it which makes us feel that there is a moral value in work and an inherent indecorum in idleness? These, too, are attitudes not shared in countries which have not undergone the baptism of asceticism. The Calvinist seed is too deeply implanted in our traditions to be extirpated with ease; and while the attitudes it engenders may be useful, we should beware of mistaking them for universal or inevitable." This unwillingness of entrepreneurs to continue working in the poor countries is made particularly serious by the fact that the educational pattern and the value system of the poor countries usually severely limits the number of people who are willing to set up factories and produce goods.

The successful development of the poor countries depends therefore to a large extent on our ability to destroy the forces creating vicious circles and to bring about reactions favorable to economic growth. Until this takes place, growth will not be built into the economy of each of the poor countries. W. W. Rostow, one of the most eminent authorities working in this field, has developed this conclusion. He has shown that economic growth depends upon the pre-existence of particular social attitudes. But we are unable to wait until education has led to this change. Our crucial problem at the present time is that we must find a way to use our available material resources to help the poor countries to develop despite the fact that vicious circles will interfere with their growth.

How can these three vicious circles be overcome and how can the poor countries take steps to help themselves at the present time? First, measures must be taken to limit the rate at which desires for consumption increase, for they will cut into the amount available for investment. The rate of increase in the demand for goods is *already* so great, because of the revolution of rising expectations, that no unnecessary encouragement to consumption should be allowed. This does not mean that consumption can be kept from rising, for the revolution of rising expectations is irreversible. However, promotional expenditure and time-payment plans should be limited and the rich countries prevented from flaunting their wealth. Although wants will still continue to rise—and Hollywood films and slick magazines will add to the pressure—any reductions in the rate would be beneficial.

That this problem is a major one can be seen by the attitude of the Jamaican authorities to tourism. They recognize that it is essential if they are to maintain a sufficient rate of economic growth, but they are deeply concerned lest the high standard of living of the visitors disrupt the pattern of life in the rural areas. They are also disturbed by the severe upward pressures it has caused on the cost of living, particularly for the middle classes.

The present rate of population increase, which leads to the second vicious circle, leaves us with only two choices: either we resort to birth control or we allow a 3 per cent increase in world population. Only the first of these choices is realistic in the long run and will make possible a rising standard of living in the short run. Education should force us to try to understand and control the changes taking place in the world for the good of mankind. We cannot be satisfied until we have examined closely and clearly whether our present attitudes are justified.

Although a willingness to look squarely at this issue would help, it would not solve the problem. None of the existing methods of birth control can be satisfactory in the insufficiently educated and traditionally oriented societies of the world. Two steps must be taken if a useful program of birth control is to be inaugurated. The first is to develop a cheap contraceptive—probably oral—that does not require a strict sense of time and is acceptable in each society. The second and usually more difficult step is to make sure that the resultant contraceptive is actually used by those in the poor countries.

Failure to pay for research on birth-control methods is often justified by the assertion that the people in the poor countries will not practice birth control. Such a belief is largely based on a lack of knowledge of recent surveys. When the attitudes of the populations of the poor countries with heavy population densities and high birth rates have been examined, there is usually a very large proportion of the people in favor of family limitation, even if the religious authorities are opposed. The West cannot evade its obligation on the grounds that birth-control methods would not be used; it must spend the money required to ensure the most rapid possible development of contraceptives.

Unfortunately, money is not the only, or even the most vital, factor needed for this research. The scarcest commodity is time, and this cannot be increased. Many years will be needed to be reasonably certain that new methods of contraception will not have undesirable side effects and to reduce manufacturing costs. Thus even if a revolution in the attitudes of the rich countries could be achieved in the immediate future—a revolution that, it may be said, does not appear to be imminent—there could be no dramatic decrease in births within the next decade. Indeed the continuing fall in the death rate and the change in the age structure of the poor countries must be expected to lead to a further rapid rise in the rate of population increase in coming years.

What can be done to solve the problems raised by the third vicious circle—that people in the poor countries, particularly entrepreneurs, reduce the amount of work they do when their income increases? One proposed solution is to increase the standard of living each individual hopes to attain, for if the amount he wishes to buy rises he will be willing to work longer hours. Such a change will often be unsatisfactory, for the favorable effect of the increased willingness to work would be offset by the increased desire for additional consumer goods. Indeed, because it is not usually possible to satisfy all the existing desires of consumers, a deliberate attempt to increase wants might well raise discontent in the community to a dangerous level.

A second possibility would be to try to encourage workers to lend their money to the government for investment purposes rather than to use it for consumption. The problem with this solution—apart from the ever-present difficulty of changing attitudes—is that the process of growth in many of the poor countries will almost inevitably cause inflation. Those who lend their money may find that the sum they receive when they require it back will buy less than they could originally have bought. This is not only unfortunate from the point of view of equity; it is also a serious block to any attempt to encourage people to save their money rather than to spend it.

A third possibility is for the government to attempt to influence people to work longer hours and more intensively. There are two major ways in which this can be done. The first is by the imposition of taxation. Those who are forced to pay increased taxes may try to make good the decrease in their posttax income and therefore increase their amount of work. There is, however, always the danger that, if the rate of taxation is too heavy, people will actually cut the amount of work they do or spend a large part of their time working out how to avoid taxes.

An increase in taxes has often been proposed by the Western social scientist as the appropriate solution for the poor countries, and the adoption of tax systems similar to those used in the West has usually been suggested. Our acceptance of present patterns of direct (income) taxes has caused us to forget that our methods of taxation are largely the result of historical accident and inaccurate economic analysis. It may well be that other forms of taxation will be more "efficient" in the poor countries. For example, it might often be better to use indirect (sales) taxes, which are less obvious than direct taxes and will therefore often have a smaller unfavorable effect on the amount of work done. In addition, indirect taxes can be used with considerably more flexibility than direct taxes. Their rates can be adjusted so as to encourage the use of abundant resources and to discourage the use of those in scarce supply.

One of the main reasons why the amount of work is limited is that people do not think the rewards from work worth while. They therefore prefer doing nothing to producing goods. It is obvious that this pattern can be changed by encouraging people to consider work for their country as the most important way of spending their time. This is the second method open to the government as it tries to increase the number of hours of work each person is willing to contribute. The result of such exhortation can be a new dynamism among the people, as has occurred in Cuba, China, Guinea, Ghana, and many other areas. But as we have found to our cost, the construction of new patterns of life is usually accompanied by pressure against recalcitrants and by revolutionary fervor directed toward both interior and exterior problems. The world that results is not a comfortable one, particularly for the rich countries. We must realize, however, that the cake of custom will not break easily, and it may only be under the influence of such a revolutionary (charismatic) personality that it will be possible to change attitudes rapidly. Weber, in the celebrated analysis of types of authority mentioned in an earlier chapter, stated that only charismatic power based on personal magnetism could effectively break through precedents and previous logic. Unfortunately, it will appear to those living in other societies that the personality of the individual who achieves this breakthrough is illogical and even fanatic.

We must make the mental effort necessary to allow us to realize that revolutionary attitudes *will* often be essential if the required increase in production is to be achieved. The labor battalions used in China, Cuba, and the African states under different names are not *necessarily* evidence of communism or totalitarianism—they show that the rulers of these countries have seen that their unused labor force is their greatest available resource. We must accept that human capital will be employed to carry out necessary investment work. We must not condemn this practice as always wrong. It seems possible that the payment of some of this available labor with the surplus food available in the rich countries would increase the potential of this method and reduce some of the dangers always inherent in it.

The basic lesson for the West is that the poor countries will be able to benefit from sustained growth only if they change their economic systems and their social and political processes. None of the Western countries was forced to make changes at the rate that will be necessary in the poor countries. If we continue to denigrate their efforts—as we often have in the past—simply because they depart from the pattern that exists in the West, it is certain that the present lack of understanding between the poor and the rich will develop further. It is only if we take the trouble to understand why a state accepts a certain policy—all policies are rational at least from the point of view of those who adopted them—that the rich countries will survive the revolutionary ferment that will shake the whole world during the remainder of the century.

However large the amount of help the West may give, it is far from certain that violence can be avoided as the poor countries leave the "Middle Ages" and try to catapult themselves into the twentieth century. This should be no surprise, for the countries of the West suffered from considerable violence as they tried to change *their* social and political structures. What can the West do to help in this process? Perhaps its greatest contribution would be a minimization of economic strain by an alteration in the conventions that govern economic exchange among countries. The next chapter is devoted to this subject.

# 12.

## Economic Relations between the Rich and the Poor Countries

ONE OF THE great catch phrases of the postwar period has been "trade not aid." We have seemed to suggest that the two processes are entirely separate and distinguishable: we have stated that we preferred that countries *earn* the foreign exchange required to buy goods from abroad by trade rather than be *given* funds for this purpose. Unfortunately, the unambiguous clarity of this phrase vanishes as we examine it in the light of the insights we developed during the study of the rich countries: we find that differing methods of production and distribution in the rich and poor countries distort the gains each receives—only too often the benefit of trade accrues in very large part to the rich countries.

Neoclassical economic theory built up a remarkable structure that "proved" that the price of goods and the price of factors of production—land, labor, and capital—would reflect the relative demand for them and that this free market pattern would lead to the most rapid possible rate of growth. We saw in earlier chapters that this was not true—that labor unions and industries can use their power to increase prices: the labor unions by restricting entry and pushing up wages, and the manufacturer by curtailing his output. Thus "power" allows groups to increase their share of the national income. This analysis can be extended to cover the economic advantage received in trading between the rich and poor countries of the world. In the rich countries mechanisms exist in most industries—and even to some extent in agriculture and mining—to prevent overproduction and consequent decreases in prices: the prices of many exports are relatively high compared to the "free" market level. In the poor countries of the world, however, most exports are of raw materials or food products: the poor countries have not developed ways to keep production of these goods down and their prices up. Goods for export are often produced by a large number of people, firms and countries: none of them is willing to cut production unilaterally in order to reduce the pressure on prices caused by a glut while the development of multilateral export-control schemes faces great difficulties.

The rich countries have a further advantage in terms of relative prices. Although the various rich countries do compete with each other on the export markets, the price of goods is not the only factor considered by a purchaser when he buys. A relatively high price for goods can be offset by the promise of better service, by more generous credit terms, by cultural ties between two nations, or even social ties between two individuals. On the other hand, many of the exports of the poor countries are sold on commodity exchanges where the only relevant factor is price per unit of production. The rich countries may gain a further price advantage in this way.

Thus the very structure of trade between the rich and poor countries suggests that the rich countries will receive a relatively high price for their exports while the poor countries receive a low one; this aggravates the already-difficult trade relations between them. Prices of goods are determined not *only* by impersonal market forces—they are also altered by forms of economic and social organization. We cannot be content with the present bias in pricing, but must seek ways in which this can be overcome. Trade is not separate from aid; increased resources could probably be made available to the poor countries most effectively by developing new methods of trading that would alter the balance of economic power betwen the rich and the poor countries.

Relations between the poor and the rich countries are somewhat similar to those that existed in labor-management bargaining at the beginning of the twentieth century. At this time the power of management was so much greater than that of the individual workman that the latter was unable to bargain effectively for satisfactory wages. In order to equalize more nearly the power of the two sides to the negotiations, special legislation was passed to allow workers to join together in unions. Today the economic system gives an advantage to the rich countries compared to the poor; new trading methods must therefore be developed that will equalize the power of the two sets of countries.

Indeed, the degree of success we achieve in helping the poor countries will depend in large part on the amount of imagination employed in devising new exchange mechanisms more relevant for the era in which we live. We are certain to fail in our task of aiding development if we are content to rely on methods developed in the nineteenth century. To take one example: international trade mechanisms were largely devised in a period when internal credit was far less important than it is today in ensuring the operation of the domestic economy. While the working of national economies has been almost revolutionized by the use of credit, international credit arrangements are still limited and makeshift; where they have been formalized, they are still far from adequate for the role they should play.

Trading methods *can* be altered in order to give greater competitive advantage to the poor countries. As the income from trade will continue to be the main determinant of the foreign exchange position of these countries—at least for a considerable period—the rich countries would do most to help the poor countries by examining how trading methods could be changed in order to favor them. Each country must be able to sell its goods abroad if it is to develop and prosper. Its success will depend on the acceptance of its goods and the price it charges. The rich countries can often limit the amount of production and keep up the price they charge for their goods without losing their markets. The poor countries often suffer from a world-wide oversupply of many of their export products: when one country has been willing to restrict the growth in the supply of a raw material, such as rubber, other countries have usually expanded their proportion of world production at the expense of the restricting country.

However great the revision of trading methods might be, it is necessary to recognize that trade alone will not provide enough money in many cases. The second possible source of foreign exchange is private investment from abroad. Investors can be encouraged to build new factories or set up service industries. But present economic and political conditions are not too favorable for large-scale investment in the poor countries. Decisions about private investment are made essentially on the basis of the financial return they will yield. Such calculations will consider not only the economic return in ideal conditions but the possibility of returns being reduced by government intervention; the ability to import necessary raw materials, machinery, and spare parts; the possibility of seizure or nationalization. If there is considerable uncertainty about any of these non-economic factors, it may well be decided that the company should expand at home where possible profits might not be quite so large but where conditions are more predictable.

This, however, may not be the controlling factor in coming years. We saw that there was surplus industrial capacity in America and that many of the most urgent wants of the population had been satisfied. Even if the past rate of growth is continued or increased in America, the consequent change in production will be concentrated in the service trades rather than in industry—steel, oil, etc. The new frontier for American business that provides great possibilities for growth and profits is in the poor countries. It is in these areas that business can employ its talents doing superlatively well what is so desperately needed—increasing the production of material goods. In the next decade we may see the dangers of going abroad become less important than the dangers of *not* going abroad.

The third method of transferring resources from one country to another is by aid. The concept of giving large amounts of money from one country to another is extremely new, and it is still not accepted as a *permanent* method of moving resources from one set of countries—those which are rich—to another set—those which are poor. It was the Marshall Plan in Europe that first developed the concept of aid payments on a large scale. The remarkable success of this program, which many agree was the essential force in the recovery of Europe, was one of the major factors that led to the extension of aid to the poor countries. Unfortunately, the program for the poor countries was based essentially on an analogy with results in Europe: it was fairly generally expected that a comparable volume of aid could bring about an equally rapid rise in the standard of living. It was not generally realized that there is an immeasurable difference between restoring a country after devastation and causing development in a country where growth has not been the normal pattern.

The basic problem in Europe was a lack of the foreign currency needed to buy the machinery and goods. Trained labor forces and skilled management were available; the sole missing factor was foreign exchange. The Marshall Plan supplied this *single* element and rapid growth resulted. In the poor countries, on the other hand, the basic necessity for growth is not additional investment goods but a change in the basic attitudes of the population so that the work and saving essential to economic growth become acceptable. Aid can seldom have the dramatic effects it achieved in Europe, although it is still necessary.

By far the greatest part of the aid given since the war has been on a bilateral basis. Part of the bilateral aid has been given because some rich countries wished to contribute to the growth of poorer areas where they had special ties. The United Kingdom has given money to many Commonwealth countries; France has supported the French Community; the United States has helped Puerto Rico. The Common Market, grouping six European powers, has set up a fund to aid the poor countries that are politically associated with its members. Many aid programs on this basis have been relatively successful, for the close relationship between the donor and the donee country have made it possible to avoid friction.

However, when aid has been given to the poor countries with which the rich donor country has no close cultural ties, results have often been more harmful than beneficial. The relationship between giver and receiver has never been an easy one even for individuals. National pride and sectional interests make grateful acceptance of continuing giving between countries even more difficult. Because the right way to behave in the giving and receiving countries will inevitably be very different, controls that seem essential to the donor country may appear insulting to the donee. In addition, the need to comply with the forms of democracy in many of the donor countries has often made it impossible to meet the unexpected needs of the receiving country. Finally, many donor countries have been trying to win countries to their side in the cold war through their aid programs.

Aid has not, of course, been limited to bilateral programs. The United Nations, the World Bank, the International Monetary Fund, the International Development Association, the Food and Agriculture Organization, the World Health Organization, and many others all make funds available to the poor countries for various purposes. There is growing agreement that these programs should be enlarged. This conclusion has been reached largely because the poor countries are more willing to accept necessary limitations and controls from international bodies, where there is less fear of self-interest, than from individual countries.

We have seen that there are a number of ways in which the amount of resources available to the poor countries can be altered. An effective policy will require that we use all of them. We can bring about an alteration in the balance of economic power that determines the relative prices paid for the exports of the rich and the poor countries, we can try to tilt the balance in favor of investment in the poor countries instead of the rich, we can work out new ways to combine and increase bilateral and multilateral aid.

We must realize, however, that there are strong forces working to offset any aid we may give the poor countries. While we compile statistics on the volume of foreign aid and investment, we do not produce figures that show how other forces working in the rich countries may actually reduce the amount of resources available to the poor. We are only now beginning to understand how drastically a decline in business in the rich countries can cut into the exports of the poor. It has been estimated that the decline in the value of the exports of the poor countries during the 1957–58 recession more than counterbalanced all the aid that was made available to them by the rich during this period. In addition, cyclical fluctuations in the rich countries often disrupt the plans of companies for expansion or introduction of productive facilities in the poor countries. The construction of one very large dam in Ghana, intended to provide electricity for the processing of aluminum, has been put off on several occasions because of the surplus capacity that develops in the aluminum industry every time a recession occurs.

This is not the only way in which the forces at work in the rich countries prevent the poor from developing: the very *rate* of progress in the rich is making economic growth more difficult in the poor. At a meeting of the Society for International Development in 1960, the economist and writer Barbara Ward pointed out that the prospects of scientific and technological progress could hamper economic growth in the poor countries by making it uncertain how long an investment would remain profitable. Africa, for example, has almost unlimited hydroelectric potential, but the task of tapping it is being inhibited by the prospect that cheap atomic power might become available in the near future. Scientific and technological developments in the rich countries also have other, and more immediate, effects. The manufacture of substitutes for natural products—synthetic rubber, synthetic fibers, etc.—has cut into the export incomes earned by the poor countries. This change has in turn reduced the imports of the poor countries. Latin America's export income from goods sold to the United States has dropped by almost one billion dollars during the 1950's although the volume of exports changed little during this period.

The introduction of synthetic products in the rich countries has been justified in the past by the belief that, if a firm found it profitable to introduce a new product, the step would necessarily be beneficial for the world as a whole. We saw in Chapter 7 that this may not even be true within a single country: when we are considering the introduction of a new method of making an article in one country that will lead to the elimination of its production in another, there is a greater chance that the over-all effects of the change will be unfavorable. Let us return to the possibility of introducing synthetic coffee, which we have already discussed earlier and examine the results that would be expected to follow if production were started in one of the rich countries.

Let us suppose that a commission should be set up to study the economic effects of the production of synthetic coffee. It would find that the successful sale of the synthetic coffee, rather than the existing agricultural product, would mean not only a diminution of the value of sales from present growing countries but also the limitation and possible destruction of the value of the coffee trees and the equipment used in growing, harvesting, and preparing the beans. In addition, such a commission would have to take into account the fact that those employed in coffee growing would have to find new jobs—and that work for these people might very often not be available.

Such a commission would conclude that the development

of synthetic coffee would certainly result in a major loss for the present producing countries. In an economically rational world it would therefore require that synthetic coffee be introduced *only* if the profit from its production were adequate to offset all the losses incurred by existing interests following this change. Such a requirement could probably be most easily satisfied by requiring the producers of synthetic coffee to pay a fixed sum to compensate those adversely affected by its introduction. In the case of coffee the size of the payment for the losses to present producers might well be so large as to make the production of synthetic coffee unprofitable. Our present pattern of thinking would suggest that the imposition of such a payment would therefore have limited "progress"; in actual fact we would merely have forced the innovator to consider *all* the costs resulting from the change he wanted to make. It is true that this type of action would be extremely difficult, if not impracticable, at the present time. However, if present systems are unjust, we are surely obligated to look for better solutions.

Our present simple calculations about the relative advantages that the rich and the poor countries gain from trade are no longer adequate. The "power" of the rich countries makes trading terms favorable to them. Our greatest contribution to increasing the possibility of economic growth for the poor countries would be the development of a system that helped to equalize the power of the rich and the poor countries in setting prices on international markets.

But however great our willingness to help the poor countries, we will not be successful in a deeper sense until we know what the basic aim of our programs should be. We are hypnotized at the present time by the almost incredible difference in the figures that purport to show the income per person in the rich and poor countries. Most of our thinking is therefore in terms of a crash program of economic development that will raise the national income of the poor countries from its present low level to one that approaches more closely that reached by the richer countries of the world. But national income figures are heavily biased by the pattern of assumptions behind them. Economics *assumes* that value is the result of scarcity—when goods are abundant they will be free. Thus, as the income of a country is determined by valuing the goods at the price they bring on the market, a country with an abundance of all types of goods' would appear to be poorer than one with a scarcity of goods. The very action of the West, therefore, in defining our economies in terms of scarcity automatically overstates the value of production today.

The contrast between a "dream" island in the Pacific and the economy of America will illustrate the point. On this dream island everything required by the inhabitants is available in abundance—they have enough food, enough clothing and amusement. The value of their production would be considered practically nil if an economist were there to measure it—for they have few scarce goods and little need to exchange their production. In America most of the inhabitants have enough food, enough clothing and amusement. But although the inhabitants of America are no more contented than those of our dream island—it is claimed that the average annual income of each person is over $2500. National income statistics are not a satisfactory way of defining the standard of living in a country.

It would, of course, be absurd to suggest that the difference between the standard of living in the rich and the poor countries results entirely from statistical methods. There are large parts of the world where people do not have enough food to eat or enough clothing to wear. Nevertheless we must not try to produce a carbon copy of Western civilization in the poor countries—the patterns of life that have proved possible and relatively satisfactory in America cannot be re-created in the poor countries of the world and probably not even in Europe. Let us return once more to the subject of transportation. America developed its economy by means of the automobile; this allowed almost unlimited mobility. The construction of vast arterial highways for the automobile in the poor countries would be extremely wasteful, while the acute shortage of land in many areas would make it disastrous. Attention must be concentrated on the more efficient methods of transport. Despite these facts one of the basic elements in many aid programs is the construction of multilane highways. We will fail if we try to remake the poor countries in the image of the rich, for the patterns in these latter countries are no longer appropriate even for themselves and certainly cannot usefully serve as models for the poor countries.

The economic relations between the rich and the poor countries must not be based on outmoded economic thought: new methods must be devised to integrate the interests of both sets of countries more efficiently. We have already seen that it might be possible to limit the damage caused to the poor countries by new synthetic products that compete with their exports. The control of fluctuations in the prices of raw materials provides a second possibility. While the potential fluctuations in the price of manufactured goods are controlled by alterations in the volume of production, the price of most raw materials and food crops controls the amount of production. Thus the pattern of causation is completely reversed. In the case of manufactured goods the price is set by the producer and output is limited to the amount the market will absorb at this price: in the case of raw materials and foodstuffs the level of price depends on how much is produced.

Continuous fluctuations in the price of raw materials and foodstuffs are, however, an anachronism in an age when the great majority of prices are fixed by the administrative fiat of firms. The survival of this method of price determination can be laid, at least in part, to the fact that the economist believes free markets are the ideal system, but it is also due to the difficulty of organizing scattered producers. In addition, any attempt by one country to maintain prices for raw materials or agricultural goods often results in the loss of markets to others who are willing to sell more cheaply.

The failure of many commodity-control schemes in the past that aimed to limit price fluctuations seems to have diminished considerably the volume of discussion about their practicability in present conditions. There have, of course, been experiments for single commodities, and in some cases these have been relatively successful, but these programs have not caused the rich countries to consider seriously the repeated requests of the poor for a system covering most, or all, raw materials. It seems doubtful if this situation can be expected to continue, for business firms have an inherent interest in being able to rely on stable prices for the goods they purchase. The business firm must try to limit uncertainty. A major advance in this direction would be the elimination of fluctuations in the price of raw materials that force each company to spend much time and effort continually reconsidering its purchasing policy, in order to determine whether the alteration in prices has made it profitable to change from using one raw material rather than another.

The existence of computers and the more sophisticated approach of the econometrist to problems of price fluctuation, coupled with the necessary minimization of cyclical fluctuations in business activity, would probably make an integrated program of commodity-control schemes reasonably efficient.

However, the essential factor that makes their introduction possible is the greater availability of resources in the rich countries: increasing wealth makes it practicable to bear the cost of overproduction of certain foods and raw materials for a limited period.

A relative abundance of funds, and an unlimited commitment to support prices at the level decided upon by directors of the schemes, would make it possible to control two factors that have destroyed many previous attempts to limit fluctuations in price. In the first place, enough money would be available to make it possible to build an adequate stock of the various raw materials and foodstuffs: prices could not therefore be forced up by a sudden surge in demand. On the other hand, a sudden weakening of demand would not lead to a collapse in prices—the commitment of the management of the buffer-stock scheme to the anounced level of prices would be complete. Indeed, the need to build stocks would be a major incidental advantage, for it would bolster the prices of raw materials that have typically been slipping in recent years.

Violent changes in the prices of raw materials are only one of the troubles that plague the poor countries. A second and possibly more difficult problem is that even the relatively minor cyclical fluctuations in the rich countries in the 1950's set up a pattern of change in export earnings that is very unsatisfactory for the poor countries. As a boom develops in the rich countries, the exports and export earnings of the poor increase. The poor countries become overoptimistic and allow large orders for imports to be made. The goods ordered at this time are often delivered just as the boom ends and the poor country finds itself with increased imports just at the moment when it is least able to pay for them. This causes one of the most startling paradoxes of the present economic system. Just at the moment when the rich countries have most spare capacity and should be particularly willing to supply goods to the poor countries, the poor countries are least able to pay for them. I have suggested elsewhere that this flaw in the system could be cured in a way that would benefit both the rich and the poor countries. This would involve setting up an international fund that would create money and give it to the poor countries when a recession developed in the rich. Such a policy would help to bring the rich countries out of a recession by increasing the demand for goods; it would provide the poor countries with the products they need so desperately if they are to develop.

Further changes will be required. The world will survive only if we develop a social-security system on a world-wide scale. The pattern of transfers between different parts of the world must take into account the fact that one of the major reasons for the ease of development in the rich countries has been the comparative mildness of natural forces in these areas. Although our climate is far from ideal, we do not have to replace roads each year as they are washed out by floods, we do not have to wage a perpetual battle to stop the jungle from encroaching, we generally have a sufficiency of water. There are many areas of the world where the standard of living will continue for several decades to be lower than in the better-endowed countries; we must provide for a continuous flow of funds from the intrinsically rich to the intrinsically poor countries. In addition, the whole world will have to accept an obligation to help when natural calamities occur: insurance against a poor harvest or devastation from floods or earthquakes should be underwritten by the world as a whole.

Economic growth is essential for survival today. However, a world in which economic growth remains the only goal will sooner or later destroy itself. It is just as unrealistic to suggest that economic growth can continue at the Western pace forever as to accept the possibility of a continuous increase in population. Both can be proved to be totally unrealistic in the long run. We must learn that abundance cannot be achieved so long as we make our main goal that of an ever-higher standard of living; we can have abundance only when we develop other goals we consider more important. Simply because it is difficult to get people to give up standards of living to which they have once become accustomed, it is essential that we should begin to consider when we should cut down the rate of economic growth in the Western countries. We must recognize that the level of wealth that the peoples of the world will require will depend inevitably on the standards the West attains.

Concentration on material goods alone cannot lead to a full flowering of the human spirit; if we develop the Western attitude toward wealth in the poor countries we will distort their cultures in a way many would feel to be unwise. Elsbeth Huxley, in her book *The New Earth,* argues: "It becomes continually more difficult to sustain a conviction that the introduction of money, literacy, taxes, votes, the doctrine of work and the religion of materialism; that the suppression of cattle-raids, magic, dancing, sacrifices and indigenous justice; that the end of contentment and the beginning of *angst;* that all these aspects of civilization have made life happier and fuller for the tribesmen. When they have turned their arrows into duodenal ulcers, their *kokwet* councils into political parties, their cattle raids into football-matches, their virgins into strip-tease artists, will they be better off?" The complaint and the argument are unrealistic, for we cannot leave the cultures of the poor countries alone, but it is indicative of a growing concern among those dealing with the problems of the poor countries.

Unfortunately we can seldom stand back and examine the basic needs of these countries, for immediate problems and crises crowd in upon us. What must we do? One of the first needs is to change our views about trade and aid so that we can see that the system we live by is not immutable and absolutely just; only then will we be able to go to work to devise new methods more suitable for the age in which we live. We must also try to find ways of making aid more acceptable in both the donor and the donee countries; we must try to strip it of its unpleasant connotations, which tend to cause the economic good done by aid to be often more than offset by the social and political damage it causes. It seems highly probable that one of the best methods of bringing about this result may be to give a considerably greater proportion of the aid through international bodies.

We must also find ways to make sure that funds are used for constructive purposes, that large proportions of them do not go to swell private fortunes. The problems in this area are greatly increased by the fact that most aid funds are channeled through a relatively small number of hands. This situation gives those in charge of their distribution almost unlimited power. It is asking too much to suggest that politicians—or indeed most human beings—should not take advantage of such a situation: patronage and corruption have almost always followed the unrestricted control of funds. Just as long as politicians felt free to distribute jobs and money in the West, the problem of patronage remained acute. There is an urgent need for new political thinking in this area. We must develop new instruments by which funds can be transferred from one country to another while avoiding concentration of these funds in a few hands.

One possibility would be to increase the flow of private investment into these areas. At first sight it would appear that

American investment in the poor countries has been considerable, for corporate investment abroad has more than tripled since 1946 and reached almost $30,000,000,000 by the end of 1959. However, Brendan Jones, in a New York *Times* article, estimated that only $1,400,000,000 was invested in Africa and Asia in 1957 and that most of this was in the extractive and trading industries.

It would be unrealistic to underestimate the changes that would have to take place in both the rich and the poor countries if investment on any large scale were to take place. Continuation of the trends operating in 1960 will almost certainly lead to a diminution rather than an increase in private investment in the poor countries. There is a growing danger that governments, when unable to obtain the funds they require by conventional means, will resort to the seizure of foreign property. The recent example of Cuba, coupled with the relative inability of the American Government to demand compensation and still conserve support for its policies in the world as a whole, has shown how politically attractive confiscation can be. And even when the poor countries are politically friendly and seem certain to remain so, the economic uncertainties involved in the present conditions must cause companies seeking profit to hesitate. There can be no certainty that it will be easy or even possible to obtain the necessary permission to import raw materials or spare parts when required. There may sometimes be difficulty in arranging for the repatriation of capital: labor laws designed to ensure maximum employment and a "fair" wage rate may seriously limit profits. These conditions may well cause the return on capital to be not much greater than could be obtained in far safer conditions within the rich countries. Nevertheless, as we saw earlier in this chapter, in coming years, the growth potential may well be more favorable in the poor countries than in the rich.

Perhaps the first essential is to develop a clearer understanding in the poor countries of the benefits tht private enterprise can bring even if it is controlled by foreign capital. Once it is recognized that foreign business can play a legitimate and useful role in the development of a country but that this role is not possible without a guarantee of certain minimum rights, it should be possible to draw up a convention that would delimit the rights of the state over the private firm and also set out the circumstances in which nationalization would be allowed. Such a convention would also state the obligations that the foreign enterprise accepted as general regulations for its operation. This type of agreement could probably be worked out only under the aegis of one of the international organizations and would have to be subject to compulsory arbitration.

The success of any program of private investment would also depend on a rethinking and re-examination of the proper goals for the business enterprise. It is still generally felt that the role of business is to make a profit for its shareholders, to pay a decent wage to labor, and supply goods to consumers at reasonable prices. Although social activities have crept into the operation of the firm, they are still peripheral, and when they are challenged management justifies them on the basis that they will, in some indirect way, increase the profits of the enterprise.

It may be wondered if this theorizing is really adequate. We have seen in Chapter 9 that the old stereotype of the corporation does not correspond with present conditions, both because policy is actually determined by the directors and because shares are concentrated in the hands of pension, mutual, and insurance funds rather than in the hands of private individuals. In addition, we saw that most firms now have informal "taxing" power, which allows them to collect a large part of the money required for further expansion from the con-

sumer rather than the investor. What should be the responsibility of the firm in these circumstances? What, if anything,
provides it with legitimate power? This question cannot be
easily answered, and the response depends upon the views of
society as a whole. But it does not seem impossible that the
concept of the duties of the corporation should be revised to
include a responsibility for ensuring the needed economic
growth in the poor countries. Only a slight change in emphasis would be required for this; the aim of the firm is being
increasingly considered as one of securing growth, and
thereby profit, rather than concentrating on profit as the primary goal. The aim of the firm today is the satisfaction of
wants. Its area of activity has been traditionally limited to a
single country; today the world as a whole is the relevant
geographical unit.

We spend a great deal of time talking about the need for
a political summit conference. Equally urgent, however, is the
calling of an economic summit conference that would take
up and complete the work of the economic conferences called
at the end of World War II. We now know the conditions we
face in trying to produce a viable pattern of international
economic relations. We must also realize that the present pattern is totally inadequate to meet our new problems. We
must develop a new system that will allow a more equitable
distribution of wealth throughout the world.

Whatever we may do, an intense strain will continue to fall
on the governments of the poor countries as they try to bring
about economic development. How should governments be
formed to deal with this task? To many this is still an irrelevant question: they claim that democratic government is
"right" and dictatorship "wrong" and feel that this statement
closes the discussion. They fail to realize that neither of these
terms can be adequately defined, nor do they understand that

the immense problems of the poor countries will require stricter control than is necessary in the rich countries.

Above all, they have failed to understand that there can be no real democracy without restraint. It is already obvious that the West cannot survive if it continues to give free rein to unrestricted individualism unhampered by any concern for the common good. In the poor countries, which are so much closer to disaster, this is doubly true. In the last two chapters of this book we consider the methods of government that will be possible in the poor countries, the changes that can reduce tension among the various countries of the world, and finally the ways in which the citizen of each country can be led to give his loyalty to a world government.

# 13.

## *Are Power Politics Obsolete?*

MANY IDEAS PUT FORWARD earlier in this book have challenged conventional beliefs. The remainder of this volume deals with particularly emotional subjects and suggests that theories and beliefs to which the West is sentimentally attached may have been outdated by change. In these two final chapters some of the ideas accepted as basic to our cultural heritage are challenged and some policies strongly opposed at the present time are suggested as appropriate in the far-from-ideal conditions of the poor countries. The conclusions of these chapters have not been reached lightly, nor are they set down to shock. The changes proposed here seem as if they might begin to deal with the various revolutions now at work—in particular with the fact that the world is now effectively united in that we can know about events in other parts of the world and by our ability to destroy civilization. I do not suggest that these proposals are ideal or even fully worked out; I would only argue that they suggest the magnitude of the necessary changes.

The utilitarian theory, on which so many of our economic, political, and social doctrines are still based, is a very comfortable one, for man has only to calculate what his own self-interest requires: the utilitarian theory then gives him moral support when he works toward this end. This "respectable" theory allowed many to ignore social needs and problems with a clear conscience: they could argue that while their actions were essentially selfish the clash of private interests would eventually produce the best possible results for society. Stated bluntly in this way, the theory appears not only untenable but ridiculous: we must however remember that it was extremely functional as it allowed the rapid rate of economic growth that society wanted.

We must understand that this outmoded doctrine still lies behind many of our policies, for until we have done this we are unlikely to see clearly enough to devise suitable plans for the future. It is under the influence of this doctrine that we believe that truth can emerge *only* when two political parties confront each other in periodical elections and compete for the favor of the voters. It is this doctrine that provides the justification for the ceaseless lobbying of special-interest groups, and that justifies giving most influence to those groups with most political and economic power. While the resulting system is not ideal, as we have seen in Chapter 9, it has obviously not been too unfavorable for the West: unwritten safeguards have been developed that prevent the most serious dangers inherent in the system from developing.

We certainly cannot simply *assume* that the wholesale transfer of this system to the poor countries will be satisfactory. Indeed the failure of democratic forms in many of the poor countries in recent years must inevitably suggest that Western methods of political control are not easily adaptable. We cannot be certain that the purpose of government—the reconciliation of the conflicting aims of various groups and people—will necessarily best be carried out by Western democratic means in the poor countries. Particular sets of clashing interests, for example, the conflict between the traditionalist and the modernist, the challenge of religion by secularism, may not be most easily or satisfactorily reconciled by Western democratic structures.

Western comments on the communist systems of government or the methods adopted in some of the poor countries— Indonesia, Pakistan—sometimes make it appear that we are in favor of conflict between two groups as a value in itself. In the poor countries, however, the Western concept of power is not always present: general consent is often required before decisions are taken. Each individual is concerned to promote the good of the whole group rather than trying to advance his own selfish interests. In these circumstances a unanimous decision does not necessarily prove the use of coercion —as is so often assumed—but may be evidence of a different approach to the resolution of conflict between groups and individuals.

If ethics were an exact science, it might be possible to decide on the right policies on the basis of scientific principles. However, ethics never will be either exact or scientific; political decisions will therefore continue to require compromise —the art of making the best possible arrangement between competing groups and individuals. No form of government is ideal: each of them will be imperfect. It is unwise, therefore, for the West to insist that its present system and methods of control should necessarily be taken over complete by the poor countries. They are not perfect even for the West, and they will often prove highly unsuitable in the poor countries. We must be willing to work toward the development of new systems that will be more relevant to the problems of the poor countries.

A statement on democracy by the Bureau of National Reconstruction in Pakistan is worth quoting to show how some of these countries look upon its meaning. "To limit democracy merely to a particular form of government or a system of its election is to take too narrow a view of the concept which has, over the centuries, come to be based upon the recognition of the equality of man enjoying the inalienable right to happiness as a member of society. It is a whole way of social life seeking to work for the welfare of the community through conscious group effort. It embodies both the ideals of human endeavour and the means of their achievement. And the life of any one community being essentially the creation of its particular environment it may not be the same as that of another. In consequence, there can be no single method of bringing about an organization that would effectively look after the well-being of all the differing social groups the world over. The methods must vary from clime to clime and reflect the genius of the people they claim to represent.

"The failure to recognize this fact in Pakistan led to the unsuccessful attempt of grafting a form of democracy which was alien to our soil and unsuited to the genius of our people. . . . Pakistanis do not have to be convinced of the importance of equality and the desirability of common weal. As followers of Islam, they have consciously subscribed to these concepts for the last fourteen centuries. They are clear in their mind that to give these concepts a tangible form, a representative system of government is needed. Such a system need not be a replica of either Westminster or Capitol Hill. Indeed if it is to succeed, it must be indigenous."

We can see how unreasonable the claim for an "ideal" system is when we remember that the drafters of the American Constitution decided that the election of the President should not be directly by the people but by a two-tier system where the people chose "electors" and the electors chose the President, undirected by any mandate from the people. They argued that only the electors would know whom to choose. Our present refusal to accept indirect elections in illiterate countries seems unwise; it may well be that such a system for choosing national parliaments or congresses may be more suitable than those existing in the West at the present time. Pakistan has adopted a system of this type where the peasant votes for the members of his local council—for people he knows and respects. The representatives he elects then vote in turn for the members of the next tier of government, and this continues right up to the level of the National Parliament.

Whatever system may be adopted, we must remember that it will always be possible to criticize decisions taken by the governments of the poor countries. But as the problems are usually so great that no really satisfactory choice will be open to them, it will not be sufficient merely to state that a particular decision is inequitable; it will be essential to examine whether any better one is available. In addition, because of the nearness of disaster, the poor countries will need to limit the use of controversy aimed solely or mainly at personal aggrandizement. The West has always accepted that this is necessary in time of war; we will understand the actions of the poor countries only if we realize that they consider their problems so grave that they must develop an overwhelming sense of "national purpose" in order to overcome them. This will often require some degree of central direction.

Our attitudes toward international affairs hardly fit us to deal with existing complexities. Over one hundred sovereign states confront each other on a steadily shrinking globe, the destiny of all of them being inextricably bound together by the power of ultimate destruction now possessed by the United States and Russia. Their various needs and cultures will force them to adopt contrasting policies and to accord differing priorities to particular goals. Violent clashes must therefore be expected between the interests of various nations and also between the citizens of one country and the government of others. Such clashes would be inevitable even with the greatest good will; with the present level of distrust the dangers of conflict are greatly enhanced. How are we to develop a transnational agreement—that will rise above national interests—rather than seek only international discussion where progress will be blocked by the fact that each state is interested almost exclusively in its own welfare?

In Chapter 9 we saw that we could differentiate between disputes that were solved by the use of power, those solved by compromise, and those solved by law. *Within* Western countries the role of law and compromise is limited: power enters into the solution of most disputes. This continuing employment of power as a method for resolving disputes even within countries must give pause to those who hope for the universal rule of world law. If it has not proved possible to reconcile the interests of conflicting groups *within* a country under the law, it is difficult to imagine means being found to reconcile the enormously greater differences between countries by these means in the near future. Despite this fact, methods must be found to compromise differences, for decisions based on power now threaten the obliteration of mankind.

What should be the way ahead? It would seem that we must look for ways of finding a solution that will be acceptable to all parties. The peoples of the world are in the process of learning that force can no longer be used even as a last resort, for the use of force would mean mutual destruction. But we have not understood that the removal of force as a possible ultimate weapon makes "bargaining from strength" meaningless. A threat has no relevance if neither side can believe it will be carried out. In labor-management bargaining the sanction behind the bargaining process is the willingness of the union and management to accept the loss that would result from a strike. In the same way the ultimate method of evoking concessions in international affairs has been the threat of war.

This threat can no longer be used meaningfully: mankind will have to learn to negotiate in the "ideal" sense defined in Chapter 9. We will have to learn that negotiation demands compromise between the views of individuals, classes, and nations whose interests do not coincide and that neither side will ever be able to obtain *everything* it wants. Instead of each party to the negotiations seeking exactly the treaty or bargain it would like for itself, they must search for a compromise that will be acceptable to all of them. The relevance of this argument is shown by the fact that many experts who have followed the progress of the arms negotiations in the years since the war agree that neither the Russians nor the Americans have ever negotiated in this meaningful sense. President Kennedy's inaugural speech was notable for its acceptance of this point of view. "Let both sides, for the first time, formulate serious proposals for the inspection and control of arms." Each side has presented proposals they knew the other could not possibly accept. Neither side was interested in a compromise; both hoped to improve their own national position at the expense of the other. It can hardly be considered surprising that little progress has been made under these conditions. Until we realize that nations cannot hope to secure their position through the use of force or power in the modern world, we cannot hope to move toward a transnational community of nations.

Rapid progress toward a resolution of conflict is not likely unless the double standard now applied to the actions of one's own country and to those of others is broken down. While all countries *claim* that they would like to order international affairs upon moral grounds, they will often argue that the security of their *own* country requires that moral rules should sometimes be broken. However, when comments are made on the affairs of *other* nations, the fact that fear of destruction will necessarily override moral principles is not generally recognized.

The U-2 incident, when an American plane was shot down over Russia as it tried to collect military information, demonstrates how this double standard can confuse the issue, for not only did America say that the flight was necessary, there was also a suggestion that it was justified. Leaving aside the series of blunders that were committed by the administration in its presentation of the United States case (for these are now generally admitted), let us consider the more basic issue of whether the United States was justified in being shocked, or even surprised, at Khrushchev's reaction during the Paris summit conference, which immediately followed the shooting down of the American plane. We must ask what would have occurred if a Russian spy plane had ben brought down over the center of America and the Russians had admitted that it was on a photographic reconnaissance mission. It seems quite conceivable that American public opinion would have forced President Eisenhower to maintain an equally intransigent front. In our preoccupation with the "totalitarian" nature of the Russian system we tend to ignore the fact that *all* regimes must take note of public opinion, that neither dictatorial nor democratic leaders can ride roughshod over the views of their people.

One of the basic requirements if we are to move toward a world comity of nations is that we should realize that the leaders of all countries are exposed to internal pressures to which they must yield if they wish to remain in office. The development of a steadily increasing degree of co-operation among the countries of the world depends upon acceptance of this fact. Each country must accept that the freedom of other nations is limited by the views of its people, and must keep itself informed of their aims and resources. A state that recognizes only those countries it approves of isolates itself from the flow of information necessary if it is to protect its own interests. In a world where conflict is impossible, accurate and complete information will be one of the major sources of power. Each country should try to understand all the potential sources of conflict of its own interests with those of other countries and constantly seek to compromise the differences.

Only if we have full knowledge of the aims of each country will we be able to seek a possible compromise. We must strengthen our diplomatic services and recognize that an ambassador should not only serve as a transmitter of messages from one country to another but is the first line of defense against misunderstanding. In many cases personal contact between the ambassador and the foreign ministry may suffice to resolve conflicts when the interests of two countries do not diverge too greatly or where their views are united by a common alliance against another country or group of countries.

It is to be expected, however, that there will be many occasions when two states will be unable to settle their differences on a bilateral basis. How far can relations among states be subject to control according to the rule of law and to what extent can disputes be arbitrated on the basis of "equity"? The World Court is available to settle conflicts among sovereign states on the basis of international law and treaty. However, little use has been made of the Court. Many authorities suggest that states are unwilling to argue the validity of their "sovereign" actions in a court of law. In addition, international law is still rudimentary and fails to cover directly many problems that might arise. A second method of settling disputes is through conciliation or arbitration. The division of the waters of the Indus Valley was settled in this way with the aid of the good offices of the World Bank. Queen Elizabeth of England was asked in 1960 to arbitrate on the exact position of the border between Chile and Argentina.

Arbitration is theoretically based on a desire for compromise on the part of both participants. In actual fact, however, many arbitrated settlements have rested more on the conclusions by arbitrators as to the amount of power each party could bring to bear than on the inherent justice of the case of one party or the other. Indeed, the use of power to influence discussions has been practically universal in the past whatever the "formal" theory on which they have been based.

Recognizing the need for new methods of negotiation and compromise, the United Nations was set up at the end of World War II. Unfortunately, the United Nations has been drawn into the vortex of struggles among states and, in particular, into the conflict between East and West. At the present time the decisions of the United Nations are not usually based on a desire to produce the best possible compromise for the conflicting powers. The votes taken on issues represent predominantly the strength of the opposing powers and many resolutions are set up in an attempt to gain propaganda victories rather than to improve the situation. Thus, although a large part of the public still considers that the success or failure of a resolution in the United Nations demonstrates whether it was "right" or not, we must recognize that its passage or rejection at the present time is largely the reflection of the power position of various countries.

If this were not true, the concern of the Western powers about present developments in the United Nations would be hard to understand. A very large number of African states were admitted to the United Nations in 1960, and there was much discussion of the possibility that the Western powers would therefore no longer be assured of a two-thirds majority within the General Assembly of the United Nations. The wording is significant. The Western countries do not argue that the operation of the United Nations will necessarily be blocked—they are distressed because they may be unable to enforce the acceptance of their *own* particular views by the Assembly. Few commentators in the Western countries have suggested that the removal of the automatic majority of the West and a willingness by the neutral countries to judge situations on their merits could be a positive advantage for the world. It has seldom been argued that this development might allow decisions to be based more closely on the best possible course for the world as a *whole*. This is not to suggest that, while present conflicts continue, decisions in the United Nations can be expected to be based on the merits of the case. Only a complete change in attitudes would make United Nations resolutions reflections of real world needs. The possibility of such a development is examined in the next chapter.

The conflict over the recognition of Communist China also gains much of its force because it would probably require the replacement of Nationalist China in the Security Council. Nationalist China, the present member, almost inevitably votes with the Western alliance and against the communist bloc. Communist China, given the present division of the world, would almost inevitably vote for the Russian bloc. The Western countries are afraid of the change because it would weaken their voting position.

It is clear that the moral support supposedly supplied by a resolution in the United Nations is largely illusory as long as votes are not secured on the basis of the rights and wrongs of the case but following pre-existing political allegiance. During the 1960 election Henry Cabot Lodge made the lack of moral justification inherent in a United Nations resolution clear when he argued that the high prestige of the United States had induced nations to support her over the U-2 incident in the United Nations despite disapproval of the American action.

What can be done to make the United Nations a more effective forum in present conditions? It is unrealistic to hope that much change can take place as long as the United Nations is dominated by cold-war issues. It is only when countries are willing to use the United Nations to help them to work out a *compromise* between conflicting interests that it can have a major effect on world tensions. This, in turn, requires an acknowledgment by all nations that there is no reason to expect that the interests of two countries will necessarily coincide—even given the greatest good will. Until we reach this position, the United Nations will not be a real deliberative body, but in the political area will remain to a large extent a sounding board for propaganda.

There are two major sources of conflict between nations today. They are the disagreement between the West and the communist powers and, secondly, the conflict of interest between the rich and the poor countries. At the present time attention is still concentrated on the first of these struggles;

it would seem that the divergence between the interests of the rich and the poor countries is likely to be far more difficult to resolve.

In the postwar years we have examined most attentively the differences between Russia and the West. While there are real and important differences, there are also very major similarities between the goals of the West and those of the communist bloc. It is sobering to remember what Prime Minister Nehru of India said when he left New York after the 1960 session of the General Assembly. "Of all countries, the United States and the Soviet Union are nearer to each other than any two countries in the world. Both take their stand on technology and what I call the machine civilization. There is no such thing as Communist technology. Engineering has the same rules to follow there and here. These are the modern things that govern the world." There is an increasing body of opinion that claims that much of the conflict between Russia and America is artificial, that the divergences between the two countries have been exaggerated while their common goals and interests have been ignored.

No such misunderstanding lies behind the potential conflict between the rich and the poor countries. The present trend is for the rich countries to get richer while the poor countries get poorer—when they do make progress, it is far slower than what is easily attainable in the rich countries. The poor countries of the world, therefore, are not able to provide the material goods needed to satisfy the revolution of rising expectations. These trends will certainly continue, even given the greatest aid and good will from the rich countries; the poor countries must be convinced that the rich countries are doing as much as possible to help them if the world is not to split irrevocably into the haves and the have-nots.

The rich countries must therefore accept an unlimited commitment to help the poor countries. If they do not do so, it seems quite possible that the problem of the relations between the rich and the poor countries—will become so serious as to endanger the Western world. Our future depends on the amount of help we give the poor countries. However, if we are to have any chance of success we must realize that material resources are not a cure-all in this situation. It is not sufficient simply to pour larger and larger quantities of money into these countries in an attempt to increase production. We have seen in Chapter 11 that the retention of stability in social relations and the avoidance of a breakdown in mental health are two of the major goals that the rich countries must keep in mind as they try to aid the poor. One of our greatest needs is to develop new institutional structures that will reflect, rather than distort, the needs of the world. The last chapter of this book is concerned with methods of providing such institutions, and with the possibility of developing a sense of commitment to the world as a whole.

# 14.

## World Citizenship: Dream or Necessity?

WILL WE EVER come to regard ourselves as citizens of the world and give our loyalty to all of humanity rather than to a single section of it? This could come about in two ways. We may abandon the concept of national citizenship because the pattern of events makes this step essential: problems may cease to be soluble using the concept of national sovereignty. Secondly, there may be a change in the ideals of the peoples of the world so that the concerns of other countries come to appear as important as those of one's own. In short, we may either be *forced* to adopt or *wish* to adopt the concept of transnational citizenship.

A cursory glance at the present situation would undoubtedly lead to the conclusion that the concept of national sovereignty and power is more strongly entrenched today than

216

it has ever been in the past. We will find, however, that events are conspiring to force reconsideration of present ideals and that there is a considerable ground swell of public opinion holding that a commitment to the world as a whole is the only possible pattern in today's interdependent world.

We saw in the last chapter that the present approach to international order was postulated, in the last analysis, on the possibility of using force—on the ability of one country to use power to enforce its demands. We also saw that this power was now largely illusory because neither of the great powers can afford to provoke the other to a point where it will use its ultimate deterrent—its nuclear arsenal. The events of 1960 showed just how far the possibility of using power has diminished.

The summer of 1960 saw a threefold crisis examined in the United Nations: the relations of Cuba with the United States, the collapse of civil order in the Republic of the Congo, and the shooting down by the Russians of an American plane—the RB-47. The Russians claimed that the aircraft had flown over Russian territory, the Americans that it had been shot down over international waters. As East-West relations had reached a low point following the collapse of the summit conference in May 1960, each of these issues became part of the cold-war pattern. The RB-47 was, of course, directly involved: Cuba suffered economic sanctions imposed by the Americans; Russia and China came to her aid through purchasing sugar and supplying oil and other essential goods: the possibility of intervention by the major powers hung over all the negotiations in the Congo.

The Cuban problem perhaps best illustrates the problem of the great powers today. America's first reaction to Premier Castro's overthrow of Batista's dictatorial regime was approval—a hope that Castro would help Cuba to achieve the rate of economic growth needed. Unfortunately for Cuban-American relations Castro considered that any program that would lead to an adequate rate of growth had to include steps damaging to the interests of American landholders and industries—along with those of the large Cuban landholders and industrialists.

American protests over these policies set up a chain reaction that will probably change Latin-American history. The United States not only argued that Castro was attacking its interests but also claimed that Castro was breaking international law—or at the very least was violating accepted canons of good behavior. The United States seemed unwilling even to consider the possibility that progress would be possible only by breaking some of the accepted economic conventions.

This pattern of American reactions led to a widespread suspicion in Cuba that America was trying to sabotage the revolution: the growth of this view made further anti-American actions almost inevitable. This, in turn, led the Americans to study whether sanctions should be applied against the Cuban Government and eventually to the cancellation of the Cuban sugar quota in the summer of 1960 and an embargo on many types of exports in the fall of the same year. The result was predictable. As America and Cuba became more estranged, Russia and China took their opportunities and offered to supply Cuba with goods. Thus America's policy succeeded in driving a potential friend into closer and closer relationships with the communists. Even an anti-Castro revolution, which many hope for as a result of these actions, would not undo the harm that has been done: if indeed such an event would not aggravate further the Latin-American situation.

The irony of the situation is that both Russia and America will have less and less freedom of action if they both continue to accept the basic postulates on which the East-West struggle is apparently to be waged. Each of them must be willing to support any country that turns to them for aid, for unless they do so they will lose a potential ally. Thus it is the poor countries that have relative freedom today, for they can play one side against the other.

While the Cuban situation demonstrated the relative impotence of America when her interests were damaged, the case of the RB-47 showed a growing sense of cynicism toward the actions of both the great powers. During the discussion of this problem in the United Nations it became evident that both sides in the cold war were engaging in the hazardous pursuit of sailing and flying close to the shores of its rivals in an attempt to discover what the other was doing. The New York *Times* expressed the attitudes of the neutral members of the Security Council in the following words. "The day's debate revealed considerable reluctance among the members of the Council to accept either the Soviet charge that the United States plane had violated Soviet air space or the American denial."

The real revolution occurred when the Belgian Congo became independent. Within days civil order broke down and violent unrest occurred throughout the country. Neither power bloc was able to act effectively, and the United Nations organized the dispatch of a force that grew to some twenty thousand men. The mechanism of a world police force, which the great powers have consistently refused to discuss, had to be produced on an emergency basis, as it had been before. It has become obvious with the crises of the Suez, Lebanon, and the Congo that the intervention of the United Nations will be necessary to avoid certain types of conflict. We cannot afford to tackle each crisis on an *ad hoc* basis, but must provide adequate machinery so that troops and support will always be available.

It would be thoroughly unrealistic to contend that the United Nations is ready to assume this responsibility. All the dangers of the United Nations actions came to the fore during the Congo operation. The various members of the United Nations took sides and tried to advance the interests of those they supported. As a result, the effectiveness of the United Nations operation was gravely threatened.

The United Nations is very seriously hampered by the fact that the highest loyalty at present generally recognized in the world is to a nation state: each individual is brought up to swear to defend his country against all enemies, and all he reads and learns combines to reinforce him in this view. Almost all the media of communication present the news from the angle of a specific country and its interests: many businessmen are most concerned with their interests within a single nation state. The survival of the nation is naturally given top priority by its officeholders.

In these circumstances any suggestion that there may be interests higher than those of the individual nations must automatically seem treasonous, for such an attack seems to challenge the survival of the state itself. Thus there will be considerable pressure against people who advocate policies *un*favorable to their own countries even if the policies should be wise for the world as a whole. In the same way, in an earlier age, the feudal chief had to react violently if some of his followers became infected by nationalism, for they became unreliable; if the feudal lord was challenged by the king, he could no longer be sure that his followers would remain loyal.

The process of creating nation states resulted in a period of struggle that decimated the population of Europe; the shift in loyalties led to a semi-permanent state of conflict. It is only too obvious that, in the absence of the ever-present threat of the hydrogen bomb and other methods of chemical and biological warfare, conflict would again be endemic today, for there are no adequate methods of ensuring peaceful settlements of conflicts. The situation is the same as that in earlier centuries when the rules for avoiding conflict between feudal chiefs were insufficient. In the same way as the increased interdependence of different parts of a country made permanent conflict within it intolerable in earlier centuries, so the increasing interdependence of the world as a whole has made conflict between sovereign states impossible if the world is to survive. The existence of the hydrogen bomb has averted most open conflicts in the 1950's but only at the cost of a level of tension in world affairs that is in itself a constant and growing threat to the preservation of peace. The survival of man depends upon our ability to recognize the need for a limitation of sovereignty and to discover ways of creating policy on a transnational level.

This will be possible only if people are willing to start examining problems from a transnational rather than a national point of view—to give their allegiance to the world as a whole rather than to a single country. We have failed to realize that a policy that looks adequate and even satisfactory from a national angle may be stupid and even destructive when regarded from the point of view of the world as a whole. Each nation must accept that the fate of all countries is now interconnected and that only recognition of this fact can allow the world to survive. Loyalty is often an unreasoning emotion, expressed perfectly in the statement common in the early part of the twentieth century: "Our country, right or wrong." We can no longer afford this form of parochialism.

There are already a number of people for whom the concept of the national state no longer makes sense. Many of

them were brought up under the influence of several different cultures. They have accepted the fact that each society has
its own vices and virtues and its own particular interests—
they realize that in present conditions the interests of the
world as a whole must be given primacy. This does not mean
that they have necessarily ceased to feel affection or even love
for their home country—it only means that they are willing
to examine the statements and actions of their own nation
with the same critical judgment as they accord to those of
other countries. Other people have reached this position as a
result of an intellectual examination of the situation, by emotional commitment or following travel in different countries.
All of them, however, find it difficult to get wide circulation
for their views. Only with the formation of a group of world
citizens owing their allegiance to the world as a whole and
not to a specific country can their ideas be given fully meaningful expression. Those adopting world citizenship would
subordinate their commitment to their own country to their
commitment to the world.

The nature of a change from owing allegiance to a country
to owing allegiance to the world as a whole is still gravely mis-
understood. We can comprehend it better if we look at the
process that has occurred as loyalty has moved from a geographical locality to a country. Those who have accomplished
this transition have accepted that their interest in the place
where they were born or where they live must necessarily be
transcended by their loyalty to the country as a whole. This is
not primarily a process of destruction but a process of addition. In the same way, the person who accepts world citizenship will retain a loyalty to his nation but will realize that his
commitment to the world as a whole has priority. This
change does not demand, as is sometimes suggested, a complete reversal of the previous pattern; it merely means the
addition of a new dimension.

To what extent could a nation allow people to abandon their own citizenship to accept world citizenship? On a superficial level it might appear that there should be no objection, for the laws of most states allow a citizen to relinquish his citizenship if he wants to do so. However, when the subject is examined more deeply, it is clear that the two changes are not similar. A person who changes allegiance from one country to another remains within the present system of national states and does not undermine it. He is still neatly classified *within* the system. On the other hand, the growth of the concept of world citizenship would naturally and irrevocably undermine the primacy of the nation state. The creation of a valid concept of world citizenship would require a deep alteration in present views.

What would be the advantages of the development of world citizenship? First, it would allow the growth of a forum in which issues could be discussed from the transnational point of view and not from the partial viewpoint of a single country. World citizens would know that they all shared the same common concern for humanity as a whole, and their arguments would start from this first principle rather than from that of preserving the interests of a specific country. The very existence of this group would provide those who have been unable to see the necessity for world co-operation with information that will make this point: economic and political systems could be developed in the interest of the world as a whole. Indeed, the very acceptance of world citizenship would have its importance, for it would show the number of prominent *and* unknown people who believe that only through changes in the pattern of loyalty can mankind survive.

Second, the creation of a class of world citizens would make available the personnel for a genuinely international civil service—a goal considered essential by many experts in this area. One of the major problems at the present time is the fact that many poor countries do not want or do not feel able to hire nationals of particular countries, for they associate these countries with their past colonial status. The fact that nationals of the country may have disapproved deeply of these policies obviously has little relevance for the government of the poor country. But if an expert can deliberately choose international status, the issue of past nationality will clearly be of less importance. While it would be inappropriate to insist that all those working for international bodies should take the step of renouncing their nationality, it seems clear that as the system developed this would become a logical requirement.

The third advantage would be in terms of finance. At the present time the United Nations survives on an inadequate budget voted each year by its member states—a budgetary allowance that is pitiful in comparison with the abundance of the rich countries. The creation of world citizenship would carry an obligation to pay taxes to the international organizations, and this would begin to provide additional funds that would allow greater freedom of action. Incidentally, the inclusion of responsibilities as well as rights in the concept of world citizenship would largely avoid the possibility that it might become "chic."

It is clear that the contribution to United Nations finances by world citizens in the early stages of the scheme would be of greater psychological than practical importance. However, it remains true that the rate of progress that can be attained by the United Nations will be determined in large part by its ability to raise sufficient funds to support its necessary activities. Owing to the failure of certain countries to pay for emergency operations, the United Nations' finances have long been dangerously close to exhaustion. As long as each national treasury holds the purse strings and as long as each treasury suffers from an acute shortage of funds, it seems unlikely that the United Nations will be able to increase its activities at the required rate.

There seems to be four possible developments that could be helpful in this situation in addition to the money received from taxes on world citizens. The first possibility is that voluntary giving to the United Nations will be rapidly extended throughout the world; this choice could be adopted by those who do not want to renounce their citizenship but who acknowledge the importance of the United Nations in today's world. One group of Quakers agreed, for example, that they would pay 1 per cent of their income to the United Nations for the preservation of world peace and order. The document in which they announced their decision deserves quotation.

"Man's scientific genius has reduced the world to one geographic community in which all men are neighbors, but politically the world remains divided into conflicting, competing and war-threatening groups.

"In truth, man's scientific inventiveness has so far outrun his political and economic development that man's hopes for a creative life and a measure of well-being seem threatened with mass destruction.

"We feel the welfare of each person who dwells on this earth has become interdependent with the welfare of all others. Out of this sense of interdependence, we feel a measure of individual responsibility to state some of the conditions we believe are required for world peace and to take some action, however small, to help bring these conditions into being.

"We believe that men must consent to be taxed and governed by a system of world law that can maintain peace in the world community which science has brought into being. We believe that this law must be enforceable upon the individual citizen. Further, we believe that if peace is to be accompanied by justice, the grave economic disparities which presently exist betwen peoples and nations must be reduced and gradually eliminated through generous sharing on the part of the more economically privileged citizens of the world community.

"On this United Nations Day, October 24, 1959, we hereby voluntarily tax ourselves one per cent of our gross income for 1958 and give this tax as a gift to the United Nations, the one tangible symbol of world community, imperfect and incomplete though it may be.

"We wish this self-imposed tax to be a token not only of our willingness to be taxed and governed by a system of world law but also of our desire to share in the economic betterment of other peoples and areas.

"Peace through world law today remains a vision, but we dare to believe that just as men of science have opened new frontiers in time and space, so men of good will can create new political and economic patterns to achieve a world community in which men are at peace with one another."

A second suggestion that deserves consideration as a method of increasing the amount of funds available to the United Nations is that the countries of the world should pay a small percentage of their national tax yield from all sources to the United Nations and other multilateral bodies. Such a percentage might perhaps start at one fourth of one per cent and work upwards over a period of years. Having discussed, however, the problem that even the rich countries face in rasing sufficient taxes—a problem even more acute in the poor—it may be doubted if this program has much chance of political acceptance. A third possibility is that we should apply a "process" tax, that is, a tax raised as part of the process of the world economy (the meaning of a process tax was more fully discussed in Chapter 5). The exact method that could be used on the international level would have to be thoroughly discussed, but it seems that a small tax on all international transfers of money would be a possibility.

Finally, it might be possible to give the United Nations power to create money on the international level in the same way as the rich countries create funds in their countries. As long as all the resources within the world are not being used, it is possible to work out new methods that would allow the employment of the unused resources. There are several different methods that could be used to ensure that the United Nations gets enough money to operate effectively. Each of them will require a willingness to look at unfamiliar possibilities without prejudice and to explore solutions that either have not been used in the past or have been rejected as unsuitable.

The United Nations' success will depend upon a revolutionary change in existing attitudes toward the world and on a willingness of governments to allow such a revolution to take place. The prospect of bringing about such a change may seem minimal to many readers. I can only agree. There is no precedent to suggest that changes of this magnitude can be carried out peacefully. In the past, when a social system had become inappropriate, only violence was able to dislodge those groups benefiting from the illogicalities of the system. An observer from outer space would certainly give odds of three to one that we will have blown ourselves up by the end of the twentieth century.

It is this very fact—as has often been observed before—that gives us hope: mankind has never confronted a situation in which failure would mean destruction of the whole world.

More important, however, is our increasing self-analysis, our humanness. We have become aware that we can analyze the future course of events and can predict what will occur. With this knowledge comes the realization that by changing our actions we can alter the course of history. There is considerable and growing support—although it is still largely latent—for revolutionary changes that will allow us to live in the conditions we have ourselves created. We cannot be sure of success but we can be sure that if we do not make an effort we shall fail.

# Bibliography

This is a personal bibliography that makes no claim to completeness. Its object is to suggest a very limited list of books and other publications that have seemed helpful or challenging to me. The bibliography is divided into three parts, corresponding to those of the book; certain volumes, however, could have been placed in two or even all three.

## PART I.  THE ECONOMIC CHALLENGE

Daniel Bell. "The Subversion of Collective Bargaining." *Commentary*. March 1960.
>    Wage negotiations: their rationale and their reality.

Kenneth Boulding. *The Image: Knowledge in Life and Society*. University of Michigan Press, Ann Arbor. 1956.
>    A first step toward reintegrating the social sciences.

Harrison Brown, James Bonner, and John Weir. *The Next Hundred Years*. Viking Press, New York. 1957.
>    Looking beyond today's crises, the authors consider the possibilities of supporting greatly increased production and population.

Ralph J. Cordiner. *New Frontiers for Professional Managers.* Mc-Graw-Hill, New York. 1956.

> The present president of General Electric attempts to set up valid aims for a corporation in a changing world.

*Fortune. Markets of the Sixties.* Harper & Brothers, New York. 1960.

> Gives statistical and factual evidence of the changes the sixties will bring.

John K. Galbraith. *The Affluent Society.* Houghton-Mifflin, Boston. 1958.

> The general realization of the immediacy of the problems raised by increasing wealth in America stems largely from this book.

John Maynard Keynes. *The General Theory of Employment, Interest, and Money.* Harcourt Brace, New York. 1936.

> The book that revolutionized economic thinking in the West.

C. Wright Mills, editor. *Images of Man: The Classic Tradition in Sociological Thinking.* George Braziller, New York. 1960.

> Selections from the works of the great—mainly nineteenth-century—social commentators.

Charlton Ogburn, Jr. "America the Expendable." *Harper's Magazine.* August 1960.

> A challenge to the belief that the economic forces at work in America will produce the "good" society.

Stanford Research Institute. *Possible Nonmilitary Scientific Developments and Their Potential Impact on Foreign Policy Problems of the United States.* Produced for the Committee on Foreign Relations, United States Senate. 1959.

> Documents some of the effects of the scientific revolution and discusses their implications for the economy and society.

The President's Raw Materials Commission. *Resources for Freedom.* Government Printing Office, Washington. 1952.

> Although somewhat out of date, it remains the best complete reference source on America's supply of and demand for raw materials.

PART II. THE SOCIAL CHALLENGE

Chris Argyris. *Personality and Organization: The Conflict between System and Individual*. Harper & Brothers, New York. 1957.

A systematic and integrated approach that makes suggestions for ending the often-present alienation between the individual and the organization.

Jacques Barzun. *The House of Intellect*. Harper & Brothers, New York. 1959.

An examination of the uses of intellect: it tends to treat intellect as important in itself rather than as one way of helping to solve man's problems.

Francis Bello. "Great American Scientists: The Biologists." *Fortune*. June 1960.

The contribution that biology may make and the problems it may cause in coming years.

William N. Chambers and Robert H. Salibury, editors. *Democracy in the Mid-Twentieth Century*. Washington University Press, St. Louis. 1960.

An "effort to stimulate a more satisfactory concept of democratic values."

John Dewey. *Freedom and Culture*. G. P. Putnam's Sons, New York. 1939.

The conditions for freedom in the modern world.

Peter F. Drucker. *Landmarks of Tomorrow*. Harper & Brothers, New York. 1959.

Where are today's social and economic currents taking us?

René Dubos. *Mirage of Health: Utopias, Progress and Biological Change*. Harper & Brothers, New York. 1959.

The results of present economic and social trends on our health—both physical and mental.

Alan Harrington. *Life in the Crystal Palace*. Alfred A. Knopf, New York. 1959.

Study of business and personal relations in a modern American firm.

Robert Redfield. *Talk with a Stranger*. Fund for the Republic, New York. 1958.

A brief, brilliant essay on the issues that the development of abundance has raised.

David Riesman and others. *The Lonely Crowd.* Yale University Press, New Haven. 1950.

The relation of the individual to society in America.

Rockefeller Brothers Fund. *The Pursuit of Excellence.* Doubleday, Garden City. 1958.

United States educational needs in the latter half of the twentieth century.

J. A. Schumpeter. *Capitalism, Socialism and Democracy.* Harper & Brothers, New York. 1942.

One of the best discussions of the forces affecting the development of the rich countries.

Benjamin M. Selekman. *A Moral Philosophy for Management.* McGraw-Hill, New York. 1959.

The way in which the economic imperatives of the firm and the moral imperatives for the individual can be reconciled.

C. P. Snow. *The Two Cultures and the Scientific Revolution.* Cambridge University Press, New York. 1959.

How to integrate the humanitarian and scientific needs of the community.

William H. Whyte. *The Organization Man.* Simon & Schuster, New York. 1956.

The threat that institutionalized conformity poses to the development of a satisfactory community.

PART III.   THE INTERNATIONAL CHALLENGE

Thomas Aitken, Jr. "The Double Image of American Business Abroad." *Harper's Magazine.* August 1960.

Despite the material benefits that business interests from outside countries may bring, they are often resented. This article makes suggestions for the minimization of unfavorable effects.

Gabriel A. Almond, James S. Coleman, and others. *The Politics of the Developing Areas.* Princeton University Press, Princeton. 1960.

A "functional" study of political systems in the various areas of the non-communist world.

Chester Bowles. *Ideas, People and Peace*. Harper & Brothers, New York. 1958.

The problems of the poor countries and the possibilities for a "creative American response."

Harrison Brown and James Real. *Community of Fear*. Fund for the Republic, New York. 1960.

A depressing study of some of the possibilities that could easily result from the armaments race.

Grenville Clark and Louis B. Sohn. *World Peace through World Law*. Harvard University Press, Cambridge. 1960.

"This book sets forth a comprehensive and detailed plan for the maintenance of world peace in the form of a proposed revision of the United Nations Charter."

Vera M. Dean. *The Nature of the Non-Western World*. New American Library, New York. 1957.

What are the distinguishing features of the non-Western way of life?

Clark M. Eichelberger. *U.N.: The First Fifteen Years*. Harper & Brothers, New York. 1960.

A largely factual study of the forces that have altered and will change the role of the United Nations.

D. C. Hague, editor. *Stability and Progress in the World Economy*. Saint Martin's, New York. 1958.

This report of a conference of economists discusses many problems concerned with world economic balance.

Robert L. Heilbroner. *The Future as History: The Historic Currents of Our Time and the Direction in Which They Are Taking America*. Harper & Brothers. New York. 1960.

Unhappy recognition of the fact that much of America's policymaking in the latter part of the twentieth century will be directed by forces she cannot control.

Albert O. Hirschman. *The Strategy of Economic Development*. Yale University Press, New Haven. 1958.

A challenging analysis of the need for new thinking in the study of the problems of growth.

Bert Hoselitz, editor. *The Progress of Underdeveloped Areas.* University of Chicago Press, Chicago. 1952.

A series of articles by different authorities on some of the problems in the poor countries.

John M. Letiche. *Balance of Payments and Economic Growth.* Harper & Brothers, New York. 1959.

This book, for economists, challenges the theory of international trade derived from neoclassical analysis and introduces new factors for analysis.

Wallace McClure. *World Legal Order.* University of North Carolina Press, Chapel Hill. 1960.

This book, which is designed primarily for the academic reader, explores a little-discussed subject—how world law could come to be accepted in America.

Margaret Mead, editor. *Cultural Patterns and Technical Change.* New American Library, New York. 1955.

Although one of the earliest studies of culture contact, it is still among the most important—particularly in its studies of cross-cultural regularities.

C. Wright Mills. *Listen, Yankee: The Revolution in Cuba.* McGraw-Hill, New York. 1960.

A report on how the Cuban people, themselves, see their conflict with America.

Gunnar Myrdal. *Rich Lands and Poor: The Road to World Prosperity.* Harper & Brothers, New York. 1957.

Explores the inadequacies of present economic theory and the effect of Western value systems on economic growth in the poor countries.

Julius K. Nyerere. "Africa Needs Time." *The New York Times Magazine.* March 27, 1960.

A brilliant essay on the possibility of democracy and freedom and their meaning in Africa.

Lester B. Pearson. *Diplomacy in the Nuclear Age.* Harvard University Press, Cambridge. 1959.

The effects of the scientific, political, and economic revolutions on the working of diplomacy.

W. W. Rostow. *Stages of Economic Growth*. Cambridge University Press, New York. 1960.

Develops the idea that, while the forms of political and economic organization may differ, the underlying forces will be similar in countries at similar stages of growth.

H. W. Singer. "Obstacles to Economic Development." *Social Research*. Spring 1953.

One of the earliest and best statements of the difference between the developmental process in the nineteenth and twentieth centuries.

Robert Theobald. *The Rich and the Poor: A Study of the Economics of Rising Expectations*. Clarkson N. Potter, New York. 1960.

Economic problems in the rich and poor countries and the relation between these two sets of countries.